CLOSE TO HOME

P U B L I S H E R S

BOX 3566 • GRAND RAPIDS, MI 49501

*PUBLISHING BOOKS THAT FEED
THE SOUL WITH THE WORD OF GOD.*

CLOSE TO HOME

REFLECTIONS ON LIVING AND DYING

Gladys Hunt

To my husband
Keith
whose steady, quiet confidence in God
through death's cruel forays in his life
has enlarged my life and my understanding
of the triumph of God

Close to Home

First published as *Living and Dying: A Christian Look at Death* © 1971
by Gladys Hunt

Revised edition © 1990 by Gladys Hunt

Discovery House Publishers is affiliated with Radio Bible Class,
Grand Rapids, Michigan

Library of Congress Cataloging-in-Publication Data

Hunt, Gladys M.
Close to home : reflections on living and dying / by Gladys Hunt.
p. cm.
ISBN 0-929239-16-4
1. Death—Religious aspects—Christianity. I. Title.
BT825.H864   1989   89-16969
236'.1—dc20   CIP

90 91 92 93 94 / CHG / 10 9 8 7 6 5 4 3 2 1

Seek God
who turns the shadow of death
into the morning.

Amos, the prophet

Preface

Today we buried the girl who had been my college roommate.

Yesterday I received a call from her mother, and spoke with surprised pleasure—almost too gaily—until I realized that something had happened.

She said, "We've come back from California to bury our Kathryn in Michigan. Paul and their children are here with me." I hadn't heard of her death till then.

Kathryn was dead. She shouldn't have died now. She was too young. Her children needed her; her husband loved her. Nevertheless, Kathryn was dead.

It was as if I'd died. We'd known we would die when we were older, but not now. We hadn't thought much about death, for life was good and sweet and fun, and now suddenly we weren't the invincible ones. We, the golden girls, the life of the party, the idealistic world-changers . . . it couldn't happen to us. But one of us had died. Suddenly I felt vulnerable.

I thought back over our college years and the silly things we'd done. We had been roommates three out of our four years at Michigan State, both of us journalism majors. We took a year of Shakespeare together from a funny little professor who sat cross-legged on his desk, dramatizing each character until the play lived in our memories. We went for walks and talked about life.

One Halloween we dressed up and attached ourselves to a group of trick-or-treaters, and later sat on the curb in front of our dorm eating the goodies we'd collected. We went camping, visited each other's families, and laughed a good deal. I still have the telegram she sent when she heard of my engagement.

She was my bridesmaid; I was hers. We rejoiced with each other.

We'd often talked together about God and how we could know Him. We read the Bible together. One day she came into our room, all glowy and radiant, the way a Swedish girl can be, and said, "I've met Him." And since men are often the topic of dorm conversation, I asked without much enthusiasm, "Which man is it?"

She said, "The One who lives upstairs!"

Not too orthodox a way of announcing that she had become a Christian.

The last time I visited her in her own home with her own family (a husband and three children who were awesomely like their happy parents), the Bible I had given her at the time she asked Christ to take over her life was on the nightstand by her bed. I opened it and read what I had written on the flyleaf, and all the emotion of our becoming sisters in Christ came back to me.

And so I stood by Kathryn's grave today and wept. She had so much to live for, I thought, though more to die for. My tears were partly out of wonder—that God would put me in a certain hall in a certain dorm so I could be Kathryn's roommate, and she could hear about God's Son and become one of His. I was profoundly grateful.

I wept for her mother because Kathryn was her only daughter. I wept for her children who needed her. I wept for her husband. I wept for me.

Life suddenly seemed so short.

(from my journal)

Contents

Introduction

We're on our way somewhere. Life is not accidental or cyclical. It's a journey with a destination. I like the way the person who wrote the book of Hebrews in the Bible described it. We're running a race marked out for us; we have a grandstand full of spectators cheering us on; we have a goal, a destination. That destination for believers is home.

Home is surely one of the most emotionally evocative words in the English language. Home is where you belong. It's your destination after the journey.

While traveling, my husband and I once picked up a used map. On its cover a small town was circled in red, and a line went off to the margin where the word *HOME* was written. It wasn't any place we had ever heard of, but something about the way someone had marked out this place made us feel warm inside. Home. Maybe we felt that way because of what home means to us.

Somewhere I heard the story of a missionary who had been in China for many years who was traveling back to the U. S. on the same boat with an entertainer who had been there for two weeks. When they docked in New York the missionary saw the crowd of fans on the pier waiting to welcome the entertainer. "Lord, I don't understand," the missionary said. "I've spent forty-two years of my life in China and this fellow has only been there two weeks, and look at the thousands welcoming him home and nobody here to welcome me." And the Lord answered, "Son, you're not home yet."

It's a good story because it puts life in focus for believers. We will be welcomed to our real home—our eternal home. And rewarded. We're on our way there right now. Probably closer than we think. We have to be careful not to think that the place we are living right now is all there is and get so contented that we are surprised with a change of location. There's more to life than what we have down here.

Writing about heaven, Joe Bayly asked, "What will heaven be like?" "Heaven will be my eternal home with Christ," he answered. I'll just move into the part of His Father's house he prepared for me. No fixing up that home, no parts unfinished, no disappointments on moving day. No, He's prepared it, He's made it completely ready, completely perfect, completely mine.

Whenever we discuss death or talk about dying we must put it in the context of home. It changes the subject completely. It clears our vision and lets us see more than this world. It also says how important personal faith is. God has gone to some length to tell us how to become one of His children.

"Father," Jesus prayed, "I want those you have given me to be with me where I am." Like any good father, and like the immeasurable above-and-beyond Father He is, God wants his children home.

DEATH

Death be not proud, though some have called thee
Mighty and dreadful, for thou art not so.

John Donne in *Hymn to Christ*

— • —

*T*he front of the church was adorned in traditional Christian manner for the memorial service, with one striking exception. On a platform in f r o n t of the chancel stood a pair of beautifully polished combat boots. The boots in turn supported a rifle, barrel down. A pair of military dog tags had been draped over the rifle stock and the butt was topped with a green beret. Soldiers wearing the distinctive uniform of the Army's Special Forces filled the right side of the church.

The Command Sergeant Major standing at full attention at the head of the chancel took a half step forward as he faced the congregation and began to call the roll. One after another, the men whose names were called responded from the pews:

"Here, Sergeant Major!"
"Here, Sergeant Major!"
A silence followed as if the roll call was complete. Again the sergeant major's voice boomed out, as if expecting an answer.
"Rowe, Colonel James N.!"
There was no reply. He called the name a little louder:
"Rowe, Colonel James N.!"
Again, nothing. He tried a third time, as if there must be some mistake.
"Rowe, Colonel James N.!"
But Rowe did not respond. He had been killed in an ambush on a public street in the Philippines by the communist guerrillas on April 21, 1989, a senseless murder of a man who meant much to so many.

When I heard this story of the memorial service following the death of a heroic soldier who served our country, I wept. It was partly in gratefulness for the life and commitment of Colonel James Rowe, but it was more than that. I thought of all the times when people have called out the name of someone they love only to find silence. How could someone so alive and full of ideas, personality and impact on your life now be no more? But that is what death is. Absence. A departure from this world. Silence.

Man makes a poor god. He is never more sure of this than when he dies. Worshiping at his own shrine may be a palatable experience in life; it will not suffice for death. Death strips a person naked. It is the unknown, the impenetrable. No wonder we feel uncomfortable, vulnerable in the face of so awesome an enemy—an enemy who shows no partiality for age, wealth, or position.

Poets and philosophers investigate death's mystery with imaginations of its misty fog, its darkness, its inevitability.

High school students, studying poetry units, still complain, "Why are poets always writing about death?" Death, life's great fact, compels our inquiry. I still remember an English class assignment, involving the last stanza of William Cullen Bryant's "Thanatopsis."

> So live, that when thy summons comes to join
> The innumerable caravan which moves
> To that mysterious realm, where each shall take
> His chamber in the silent halls of death,
> Thou go not, like the quarry-slave at night,
> Scourged to his dungeon, but, sustained and soothed
> By an unfaltering trust, approach thy grave,
> Like one that wraps the drapery of his couch
> About him, and lies down to pleasant dreams.

I memorized it, as directed, appreciated its imagery, but got few comfortable ninth-grade feelings from it about dying, only a sense of majestic departure. I do remember special vocal emphasis when reciting "sustained and soothed by an unfaltering trust . . . ." That seemed the most hopeful part of the poem. I didn't like the lifeless sound of "chamber in the silent halls of death." And I was aware that some violent exits from this life displayed little dignity. Did the poet really know about death?

Shakespeare comments in *Julius Caesar*,

> It seems to me most strange that men should fear;
> Seeing that death, a necessary end,
> Will come when it will come.

Francis Bacon wrote that "men fear death as children fear to go in the dark; and as that natural fear in children is increased with tales, so is the other."

They have said the phrases that have become part of our vernacular. *As cruel as death, as hungry as the grave. As sure as death. Death, that grim foe. What is so intricate, so entangling as death?* Poets speak of death's reality freely; most people do not. It has often occurred to me that, facing this great final adventure, everyone would prepare for it, knowing its inevitability. But most people don't talk about what scares them. We are more often like the man in Jesus' parable: "I will build bigger barns . . . ."

In a sense, every time death touches our lives it is a reminder of our frailty, of our temporary sojourn in this world. John Donne's words remind us that

Any man's death diminishes me,
Because I am involved in mankind;
And therefore never send to know for
Whom the bell tolls; it tolls for thee.

The toll of the bell is a call to evaluate personal values, to get perspective on our being. It can be the most constructive, enlarging and sobering of all our experiences.

Every day more than 5,000 Americans die. Seventy-five percent of these are "processed out" of crowded institutions, most of these dying without the support of a close circle of loved ones or religious faith. In the Western world many people, trusting white-coated gods in laboratories, still look to the messiah of technology for some kind of ultimate deliverance from death. Admitting that death is inevitable comes hard. Psychiatrists are now saying that death is the most important question of our time and that fear of death festers a variety of psychoses.

Increasing numbers of people now attain more than the biblical three score and ten years. Yet, at the same time, our own technology and poor stewardship of earth's bounty threatens life. Nuclear disasters potentially nullify the life-extending benefits of new cures and medicines. Some psychiatrists believe a massive panic over death pervades young and old alike in our culture. Neurosis over death, claims Dr. Rollo May, is a basic cause of psychic disorder. Dr. May sees obsessive interest in sex as a subconscious expression of anxiety over death.

> An obsession drains off anxiety from some other area and prevents the person from having to confront something distasteful. What would we see if we could cut through our obsession about sex? That we must die. The clamor of sex all about us drowns out the ever-waiting presence of death.
>
> When I strive to prove my potency in order to cover up and silence my inner fears of impotence, I am engaging in a pattern as ancient as man himself. Death is the symbol of ultimate impotence and finiteness, and anxiety arising from this inescapable experience calls forth the struggle to make ourselves infinite by way of sex . . . . Repression of death equals obsession with sex. Sex is the easiest way to prove our vitality, to demonstrate we are still "young," attractive and virile, to prove we are not dead yet.

When people reject God and His claim to raise the dead, they search for other ways to prove their immortality, for if we are not immortal our lives are without meaning. For example, a person may say, "I believe a man lives on in his children, his family or his tribal group." Or "Man may die, but nature goes on," says another who believes in a kind of salvation-through-nature—an extension of the hope of evolution. The educated humanist insists, "A man lives on in his contribution to the world in art, science, music, literature and so forth. As subsequent generations are influenced through his deeds, he is immortal." All of these are ways to assert autonomy from God.

Recently these theories have begun to leave their adherents uneasy. One well-placed bomb eliminates their hopes. Nature itself is vulnerable and in danger of being destroyed in a diseased environment. The future of humanity on the face of the earth is in question. A polluted environment, population explosion, predictions of famine, and the grim specter of nuclear annihilation make mockery of traditional hopes of immortality apart from God.

People, seeking immortality through their own formulas, find themselves backed up to a wall of despair. Nihilism, the next logical step, is a scary concept. For the young person the drug scene offers a fresh attempt to transcend life and its boundaries. How else can one return to the Garden of Eden, a garden without a serpent, a garden where life doesn't push a person, where he is free to "do his own thing"?

Steve, then a junior at a midwestern university, recalled his own quest a few years ago.

I'd look at the stars on a dark night; I'd see beauty around me in the new life of budding trees. I knew existence must have meaning, some design. But I couldn't find out what it was all about. No one seemed to know the goal of life, the meaning of being. I took a philosophy course, and that was a real disaster. The more I looked for someone who knew the answer to life, the more hopeless life looked. I couldn't find anyone who knew the way.

Then one of my friends said that if I'd get into some drugs a new world would open up for me. It would show me life as it was meant to be. He was convincing. Against my better judgment, but in desperation, I took a trip and it was bad. I was terrified. The world was distorted; I was grotesque. I was afraid—afraid of life and afraid of death.

Contemporary drama, art and literature scream out this same message of despair. The heavy rock sound in music is a noisy inquiry into the meaninglessness of existence.

If life is incoherent, what of death? If death is insignificant, what of life? Human value hangs in the balance. The mental anguish over death in the young today is unique to modern history. A mystical yearning for the supernatural, for release from the rat race of life—for hope—plagues thoughtful young people. We all have an insatiable thirst for answers to ultimate questions, whether we recognize it or not. The human spirit is not sustained or explained by scientific analysis.

"Who then will tell us whether there is any sense in living, and whether human existence is anything but a tragic—no, tragic is too noble a word—whether human existence is anything but a grotesque mischance?" asks Somerset Maugham in an essay on the philosophy of Bertrand Russell.

Out of the failure of science and philosophy to speak to mankind's ultimate need has surged a stream of superstition. Human beings, always prone to extremes, leave the shrine of rational inquiry and commit intellectual suicide at a witch's cauldron. Across the country, and indeed in the whole of the Western world, people are looking in increasing numbers to the occult, to tarot cards, to black magic for supernatural wisdom. Pollsters and fortune tellers, witchcraft and horoscopes offer the same kind of hope for a message from "outside" that a primitive people expect from a witch doctor who reads the entrails of a chicken. When a personal God, who has revealed Himself to human beings, is neglected, what other hope do people have?

Since the counter-cultural impact of the 1960s, large numbers of people have turned to Eastern thought. Both young and old have been flocking to various gurus, and even large corporations are using transcendental meditation with their employees. A turn to the East is a retreat from the rationalism of Western thought. Eastern thought is antirational and syncretistic. It appeals to people because it demands so little from them and makes truth so flexible. God is defined in pantheistic terms. The cosmos is God; there are many ways to God; the great goal is to become one with the cosmos. Individuals are only an illusion, so death is not significant because people are not significant. Anything of value just continues to go on to reach perfection. Some of these ideas have become so subtly interwoven into our culture in these intervening years that many people are unaware of the tentacles of Eastern thought. To what extent is this swing to the East another way to escape the reality of God and death?

From this philosophical climate in the mid-1970s has come a growing interest in "the weird and wonderful." Today hardly anyone raises an eyebrow at the prevalence of New Age ideas. It is a Western version of Eastern mysticism, borrowing bits from every major religion. New Agers do not believe in a transcendent God; self is god but doesn't always realize it. New Agers say that we are not our physical bodies, but are a unity beyond the body. Death only means cosmic unity. Out of this have come psychics and channelers who do large scale business in directing people's lives in tune with the universe and a great hope for a New Mankind for a New Age. Self opts to be its own god and dismisses the reality of death. The "human potential" movement finds its source in this thinking.

The Barnes and Noble bookstore at Times Square in New York City has no religious book section. Instead a section labeled *New Age* is crowded with books on the subject, probably reflecting consumer demand. It's slippery thinking.

Clergymen who have left their biblical moorings say very little about this. Questions about death are curiously sidestepped. The doctrine of "good works" as salvation is still popular in the church and leaves most people feeling uneasy, open to New Age ideas. People aren't interested in doctrine, these clergy say; they are interested in how to live. It is as if God had not spoken, as if we had no Word from Above. Does God have an answer for death or doesn't he? And if He doesn't, then who does?

It was the message of the resurrection of Jesus Christ that rocked the first-century world. The claim of the early church was not that it had a superior morality, but that Jesus Christ had been crucified and had risen from the dead. Disciples risked their lives to proclaim the validity of His resurrection and the hope offered to all His followers, "Because I live, you also will live" (John 14:19). They had seen Him die; they saw Him alive again, and that encounter gave them courage to preach about eternal life in the face of death.

This book explores the hope of those early disciples (and, in fact, of all believers back through the Old Testament) that God has prepared a home for us, an eternal glory which goes beyond our short-lived days on earth. Life has meaning and purpose now. The proof of this is that mortality will one day be swallowed up in immortality. Look where you will; there is no hope, no answer like this one. It allows us freedom to live and freedom to look at death while we are still living and know a peace which is beyond understanding.

What was your first encounter with death? Can you think back to the time when you first realized death? I remember playing "catch the ball" in front of our home one day with our almost three-year-old son. A squirrel ran in the path of a car, and then it lay lifeless in the street. One minute a running squirrel, the next a still body that could no longer run. What happened, Mommy? Death. A dog. A favorite kitten. And then a favorite person.

The way in which these first encounters fit together probably determines your present attitude toward death. Especially if someone vital in your life was involved, someone who left a huge gaping hole of sorrow. An emptiness that only disappeared when your life and mind were filled with other things. Death is hard; it is ugly. Who can explain away its awful tragedy in our lives?

I would not presume to explain away death, to write about it in such a way as to destroy its power. I cannot even explain death; no human can do that. The best we can do is to see death in perspective by looking at the realities of life in such a way that we see before and beyond this life. Perspective on death is bound up in the character and power of God. We can explain away some of life's mysteries and inequalities, but when it comes to having a perspective on death, I only know one place to turn: to God.

Death can be darkness. It can also be a "covered way which opens into light." That's why the apostle Paul could write so convincingly that we do not sorrow as if we had no hope (1 Thessalonians 4:13) and could tell us that what we see now is "but a poor reflection as in a mirror" (1 Corinthians 13:12). There's more to come.

My early experiences with death did not take away its finality or its sorrow. But I am grateful to God for letting me know people who received His grace when they needed it. My first close tie broken by death was with an aunt. I was sixteen. She had three children, one only a year old. She had a lot to live for—and she kept on living long after the doctors thought she would die. Her conflict was the human dilemma. She had a vital, personal faith in God and a strong confidence in His ability to do what was best, but thoughts of her family made life seem dear. Like the apostle, she was hard-pressed between two desires. Sometimes she prayed in her pain that she would die; then her remarkable determination to live took over and she kept on living.

My grandmother lived next door, and to isolate the family from the suffering involved, my aunt was being cared for by a nurse and my mother in grandmother's home. My cousins were too young to understand all that was happening, and even I, at sixteen, was awed by the solemnity of her pain, by her lack of recovery. A pall of deep concern seeped into our household.

When I arrived home from school in the afternoons sometimes my mother would ask me to go over and read to my aunt. Most frequently I read from well-marked Bible passages my aunt requested, and the words I read never failed to calm her restless pain. Words from hymns I had known all my life took on new meaning as I sang them to her—hymns about faith and heaven. I often sat there after she had faded into sleep and read what she had written in the margins of her Bible and wondered about life, about death, about heaven, about God—and about my uncle and my cousins. Death seemed so unreal, so scary; life seemed so sweet, so necessary.

Something happened the night she died. My mother was with her, and God did a wonderful thing for my aunt. He showed her something beyond this life. Was it a vision, a dream? She seemed rational and aware. She tried to tell my mother about it; she strained for words to describe her joy. Afterward she was content to leave this world.

Sentimental stories about death are common—often genuine and enlightening; but there will be no attempt to make this book a collection of these. I was sixteen, and when I awakened that day my mother told me about my aunt's experience and then added, "She went home early this morning." Home has always been a lovely word to me. It's a safe place. Home is the place you belong—really belong. My aunt had been earthbound. God graciously opened a wider window for her. She went home. We all sensed this, and it gave a sixteen-year-old girl new insight into death.

Was she delirious? Would she have died anyway that night? Did she see something real or did her psychological need play a cruel trick on her? However you might want to explain this, whether in belief or unbelief, it was real enough to give release and joy and peace in dying. My mother felt herself groping to see beyond; it was that real to her. With all its finality—the awful loneliness of my uncle, the stunned confusion of my cousins and all the sorrow of the rest of us—we were taken beyond the event into eternity's corridors and we saw *home*.

We need this perspective desperately. Otherwise we face life's ultimate without preparation. The only solace for some is to pretend. To think about something else. To play a beautiful piece of music. To overeulogize. It can be a way to hide. Have you ever been at a gathering where everyone is bent on keeping a new widow from realizing that her husband is dead? Talk about anything, but keep talking because death is too awful to face. Or have you known the retreating silence of those who are scared of you because you've lost a child? Not a comfortable silence, a frightened one.

That's living life on a flat plane, based on what can be seen. But hope lies in what cannot be seen here. Life is not merely physical; it is also spiritual. In a final sense our treasures are not what can be seen and handled. What can be seen is passing away. Everything earthly perishes. Only the spiritual is eternal. We know this, and yet we spend ourselves on the material. We often cling to relationships and to our possessions for security. A terrible bondage enslaves us in fear when all our well-being, all our hope, is bound up in a fading existence. To misquote Patrick Henry, "Is life so dear . . . as to be purchased at the chains of such slavery . . . ?"

Edwin Abbott speaks of this lack of perspective in his classical mathematical treatise called *Flatland*, in which he describes a world of only two dimensions, like the surface of a table. The people in this world may be straight lines, triangles, squares, pentagons, hexagons, what have you. A person's status and intellectual complexity is demonstrated by having many sides, the most perfect being a circle. Yet seeing any of these approach, others in Flatland observe only a straight line. The story proceeds to build the elements of this kind of society. Suddenly Flatland's security is threatened and unsettled. A Presence comes and demonstrates a third dimension, *space*. Inhabitants of Flatland reject and fear this concept, having lived all their lives in two dimensions. But one character *experiences* the joy of a third dimensional existence and has a whole new understanding of who he is and why he exists.

Getting a perspective on death is getting the right perspective on life. It is opening one's self up to another dimension: the spiritual. Coming to grips with death means coming to grips with God and life. We are limited by our concepts of time and space; we need an eternal point of view. Your reaction to death will be conditioned by your reaction to God. Those who are afraid of God are most fearful of death. Those who know Him well seem to welcome the opportunity of being with Him. That's the dimension that transforms death—knowing God. God has said there is more to life than we now see (2 Corinthians 4:18).

Young people expect older people to die. What hits a teenager is another teenager's death. Everyone has a kind of subconscious list of who will die before me. "I expect to die when I'm old, but not now," we say when death takes one of our peers. "Old age" is always older than we are.

The Scripture describes death in old age rather poignantly.

> Abraham breathed his last and died at a good old age, an old man and full of years; and he was gathered to his people.
>
> Genesis 25:8

Those on in years may begin to lay aside responsibility, get a smaller home, give away their treasures, or watch the obituary notices with new interest. I remember the quiet way Grandmother sat in her chair, deep in thought with the newspaper across her lap, after reading that one more friend had gone on ahead of her. "The old men know when an old man dies," wrote Ogden Nash, and it is true. The call of their peers reminds them that their turn will come soon. But even then, death surprises the living; we are seldom prepared to give up those we love.

What is it like to die? What's beyond? These are questions people ask. And not knowing the answer makes death a tragic enigma. Some say nothing lies beyond. Death is the end. Others say that God is love and if we do the best we can He will see that we have a glorious future. In answer to the first, God has said that eternity is part of mankind's genetic makeup. That's why people feel uneasy declaring the end of existence. In answer to the second, God bids us listen to what He says and not fabricate our own heavenly concepts. He has told us what we need to know and has demonstrated His reliability by overcoming death.

I've heard the wails of those without hope—the more primitive and honest displays of grief in non-Christian cultures. Their cries haunt my memories. But I've also seen death transformed by the One who walked through death and came to deliver those who through fear of death were subject to life-long bondage. It's that perspective we are seeking.

When I was a young bride I had a dear friend in her seventies. We enjoyed a good friendship. Something young in her responded to me and we shared many things together. She had a quality of life that enriched mine, and simply by being herself she influenced me deeply. In time her body ceased functioning properly and she began to fade physically. When her death was imminent, the minister standing next to her bed began,

The Lord is my shepherd . . .

My friend opened her eyes, smiled at those dear to her and, waving a farewell, said firmly,

"I shall not want."

It was a statement of conviction. And she, too, went home.

REALITY

*Walk in the light, and thou shalt own
Thy darkness passed away.*

Bernard Barton

KEITH WENT to see Tom at the hospital again tonight, but they could not talk about important things or the reality of his dying. His mother and young wife stand on constant guard and never allow any serious conversation. It's almost as if they believe their positive attitude will heal him. *Don't talk to Tom about his condition,* they seem to say. *We don't want him to lose heart.* But Tom already knows . . . .

(from my journal)

— • —

*O*n a recent Sunday afternoon my husband and I wandered across the campus of the University of Michigan to hear the University Arts Chorale and Symphony Orchestra perform Brahms's *Requiem,* surely one of the most

Christian musical commentaries on death ever written. The magnificence of the message and the music left us feeling vulnerable and strangely comforted.

Behold all flesh is as the grass
and all the goodliness of man
is as the flower of grass;
for lo, the grass withereth
and the flower thereof decayeth.

Lord, make me to know
the measure of my days on earth
to consider my frailty, that I must perish.
Surely, all my days here are as an handbreadth
to Thee . . . .

Now, Lord, oh, what do I wait for?
My hope is in Thee.

Here on earth we have no continuing place,
howbeit we seek one to come.

Lo, I unfold unto you a mystery;
we shall not all sleep when He cometh,
but we shall all be changed,
in a moment, in the twinkling of an eye,
at the sound of a trumpet.
For the trumpet shall sound
and the dead shall be raised incorruptible,
and we shall all be changed.
Then, what of old was written
the same shall be brought to pass.
For death shall be swallowed in victory!
Grave, where is thy triumph?
Death, where is thy sting?

Worthy art Thou to be praised,
Lord of honor and might . . . .

Blessed are the dead
Who die in the Lord . . . .

The triumphant *Death shall be swallowed in victory!*
echoed in our minds as we walked across campus. We felt
bigger on the inside than when we had come. We walked
along in silence for a long time, letting truth wash over us,
and perhaps each of us even facing the reality of our own
mortality. God's great and complete plan pushed us to new
dimensions of wonder and it had the ring of truth about it.
Reality is Christian, I thought, *or is it the other way
around—or both?*

One would think that, with all the shoot-outs and
violence on television and in the movies, death would
become rather commonplace, and people would be quite
practical about handling death. But the personal dimension
of death is still terrifying to most people. Death isn't a subject
for most conversations. That dread word stops people in
embarrassed silence. It's hard to face that reality and to
understand its irreversibility. After all, it is something that
only happens once and none of us know much about it.

Television and the movies actually make death more
unreal to most people. Death shouldn't be real. It's "un-
American," writes historian Arnold Toynbee, "an affront to
the inalienable right to life, liberty and the pursuit of
happiness." In *The Heart of Man*, Erich Fromm goes even
further when he writes, "Grief is sin," and gives the
psychological rationale for the repression of death. He urges
people to keep from even thinking about death. So much for
reality therapy from a prominent psychiatrist.

Death, a subject hard to talk about. Death, a devastating experience to face. Death, the inevitable. Death, my entrance into glory. How comfortingly the writer of Hebrews comments that Jesus Christ came to deliver those who were subject to lifelong fear of death.

Fear of death is no poetic allusion. Unreasonable fear grips many people who take their first flight by air, or any other adventure they feel they cannot personally control. The half-hour delay of a husband or daughter in returning home can fill the mind with uncontrollable thoughts of disaster. Fear for one's safety and well-being marks the lives of all of us. It has probably meant human survival; it has also meant human enslavement.

None of us should be glib about death. The Bible calls it our enemy; we must not hesitate to do the same. How would you react if tomorrow you found out you had a terminal illness and your days were numbered? Should a doctor tell his patient his illness is terminal? Would you want to know?

Questions like these are handled more honestly today than in the past. Doctors are human beings like the rest of us and vary in their ability to tell it "like it is," but many have found a way to combine truth and grace. Yet I have heard a wife say, "He might live several more weeks if we don't tell him. If he knows he will just give up." Sometimes family members lie openly to the dying, "No, you are not dying. You are going to be well." Reality is hard to face, but are three extra weeks of life worth such a lie? Has eternity so little to offer?

Doctors say that city people are least familiar with death and most apt to say, "Save no expense to keep him alive." Modern technology allows us to prolong our lives and our hopes. The rural person, in closer contact with the cycle of nature, is quicker to accept death as a fact of life. But increasingly in both city and rural areas, death takes place in institutions and our problems with death are due in part to the fact that we rarely see anyone die.

This is slowly changing, but our culture has attempted to so disguise death that we can't look at it with honesty. Everyone knows intellectually that some day he will die. And most terminally ill people know they are dying without being told. Some marvelous theatrics take place in hospital rooms as each pretends the other doesn't know and in elaborate conversation attempts to deceive the other. The loneliness that accompanies all this pretending only compounds the sorrow and loss.

Obviously, the Christian way of death precludes such deceit. We say that we are pilgrims on our way home, and what better time to recognize how close we are to our destination. It does not mean that a Christian will always embrace the idea of death as an old friend. But he does deserve the dignity of facing reality and finding that his spiritual resources are adequate for the demands of life.

A doctor's prognosis is always subject to the omnipotence of God. A Christian already knows this. A non-Christian needs to be given a chance to learn this—and other great truths about how to put his life right with God. We must tell the dying patient the truth in a sensible, non-alarming way. Facing death is too serious a matter for game playing. The stakes are too high.

Not only does honesty allow a person to get his relationships and personal matters taken care of, but it allows him the comfort and sympathy of a close relationship with someone who knows. Patients who are dying can feel isolated, avoided, and very lonely if the truth is not out in the open, at least with their closest loved ones. Hospice care with a cadre of caring nurses now often allows terminal patients to die at home near those they love. Such changes in our health care services take more seriously the matter of being "human."

Research done with dying patients reveals that they welcome an opportunity to talk honestly about how they feel in the face of death. But psychiatrist and researcher Elisabeth Kubler-Ross says that patients who are dying want to "hear hope." Of course they do. Hope is an essential of life. And that is just what Christian faith offers—a hope that does not disappoint. When hope is gone on earth, God, the source of hope, is still there. He offers hope for eternity. When life's realities are out in the open, this hope can be communicated. Death has ultimately been transformed by Jesus Christ.

I heard from neighbors about a young woman who was dying from kidney failure. She was terrified by the thought of dying and so was everyone else who knew her. One upsetting conversation about his woman followed another and I asked, "Who is doing anything to help her?" My question was not even understood. What could anyone do? I phoned a friend and asked him to go and visit her. He did so, and after introducing himself he asked her about herself. Very tenderly he asked, "Are you afraid to die?" She turned to him with such relief; she admitted her overwhelming fear. He had the privilege of telling her how Jesus had taken care of the ultimate pain of death. What he told her was her personal "Good News" and completely changed the circumstances of her dying.

Those who have been on the edge of death and returned have said that the last sense to leave is that of hearing. In fact, all senses seem to merge into the sense of hearing. They open their eyes and see nothing. Speech is gone. Even touch may go, but hearing is still alive. Some have commented on the conversations which took place in the room where they lay seemingly comatose or asleep. (How unwise we can be in our distress!) It is a mistake to assume that the sick person is completely out of reach. The pressure on the hand, the reassuring quiet voice can tell the dying person that a loved one is there and cares. Words are a great gift, the right words, and never more so than when they communicate hope and peace and love.

Recently a weathered woodsman from the north country told me how he had become a Christian only six months earlier. He said that when he was in his twenties, he had seen his mother die, full of faith, evidencing peace and confidence that God would receive her into heaven. He had never forgotten the witness of her life and realized that her whole life, full of hardships, had been lived in fellowship with God. Now many years later his father died—bitter, full of fear, without hope and without God. He was overwhelmed with the contrast and said, "I got myself over to the preacher's house to say I wanted to believe what mother believed because it was good for living and good for dying." Life and death are a package. The solution for the first is the grand hope for the second.

This doesn't mean that Christians don't suffer, don't sorrow, don't weep. No. Death isn't pretty. And sorrow and tears are a real part of being human. When Christians face death we simply share a perspective which takes us beyond the actual event into eternity, where God is.

We need to be better informed about death and more comfortable with its reality. We are not in this alone.

In Maria Augusta Trapp's book *Yesterday, Today and Forever*, she tells of being on tour in California. All of the family had gone, except for a daughter, Martina, who stayed at home in Vermont because her baby was due. When the family arrived at their motel in the city where a concert would be given, they found a message, "Call operator 14 in Morrisville, Vt."

It was one of those moments when the heart actually seems to stop and everything around one disappears in darkness, writes Mrs. Trapp. The message came through that the doctors had taken the baby and it had died. Then just as Martina was beginning to wake up from the anesthesia, her heart stopped suddenly. *Martina, too, was dead.*

In the days that followed the other children asked many questions, questions about death.

> All of a sudden each single one of us discovered a great many burning questions within himself . . . . Someone suggested looking into Holy Scripture for whatever answers we could find. So we divided the different books of the New Testament among us, leaving the whole Old Testament for Father Wasner. Each one was to search his portion for whatever references he could find about life after death.
>
> When we met again and each one brought what he had found on Life Everlasting in the pages of Holy Scripture, we were perfectly amazed at the amount to be found.

No human is an authority on death. The Trapp family looked to revelation for answers because that is what the Bible claims to be—God's revelation to man. And in the Book they found all the answers they needed to know. As I read of the wisdom of this family who sought answers, instead of engaging in speculation, I couldn't help but wonder why we are so slow to seek out God's answers to all of life's enigmas.

Life needs perspective if it is to make sense. *Perspective,* according to the dictionary, means the faculty of seeing all the relevant data in a meaningful relationship. What we often see around us is a mad scramble into life's adventures with no idea of how adolescence, education, marriage, the begetting of children, getting and gaining, good works and old age fit together to make a significant pattern in life. Usually the puzzle lacks the piece called death because we have such difficulty admitting that death is a reality.

Reality is hard to face sometimes, especially if the puzzle is going together badly. We are kept too busy moving the pieces into place to get the big picture. Yet the great truth is this: the pieces are easier to place when you have the whole picture in mind. Life and death have meaningful relationships. Facing both is reality.

J. R. R. Tolkien, in his great three-volume epic, *The Lord of the Rings*, with his marvelous use of language, gives us a picture of death that stirs the human heart. Aragorn, the noble king, approaches old age and knows that the span of his life-days are drawing to an end. He thus says to his wife Arwen,

> "At last, Lady Evenstar, fairest in this world, and most beloved, my world is fading. Lo! we have gathered, and we have spent, and now the time of payment draws near . . . ."
>
> Arwen, for all her wisdom and lineage, could not forbear to plead with him to stay yet a while. She was not yet weary of her days, and thus she tasted the bitterness of mortality . . . .

Facing this departure, Arwen, who is not of the world of men, has new insights into the meaning of death for those left behind: the loss and the silence. And she says to Aragorn,

> "Not till now have I understood the tale of your people and their fall. As wicked fools I scorned them, but I pity them at last. For this indeed . . . is bitter to receive."

"So it seems," Aragorn replied, "But let us not be overthrown at the final test . . . . Behold! we are not bound for ever to the circles of the world, and beyond them is more than memory. Farewell."

Aragorn insists that the time is right for him to go, and adds this beautiful phrase,

"To me has been given, not only [many years], but also the grace to go at my will, and give back the gift."

A good story always has the ring of reality, as this one does. The parting of Aragorn and Arwen admits that there is no comfort for such pain within the circles of the world. The phrases, *we have gathered and we have spent, the bitterness of mortality, the loss and the silence,* strike respondent chords within us. But more beautiful and true are Aragorn's words about "giving back the gift." Life is a gift. Eternal life is twice so. We become accustomed to it, misuse it, and take it for granted. But it is a gift, not our due. And beyond is more than memories.

TRIUMPH

Above the ruins of our lives strides the One who today advances the claim that He can authoritatively close the gap between God and man, that He can restore the world deranged by pain, unrighteousness and enmity against God, that He is more than a match for the awful majesty of death.

Helmut Thielicke in *The Silence of God*

HEAVENLY FATHER, I don't have any hope or answer besides you. Why you allowed this to happen boggles my mind; it seems so wasteful. I feel like I have a sword stuck in my middle. And yet I do know you are more than a match for death. Thank you for every time you have shown me your utter reliability. It makes it easier for me to trust you now. I have no answer but YOU. Please show us yourself and comfort us with your truth.

(from my journal at the death of Jim Worden)

— • —

*M*argaret had died of cancer the previous week. At our regular study meeting the women who had known and loved her were discussing their sorrow. We missed her; we felt diminished by her death. Two of the women in our group had prayed for her healing and were stunned. "Maybe if we had prayed more," they said.

Another woman had difficulty in coping with the fact of Margaret's death and admitted she had not gone to the funeral because she couldn't face the loss. One was glad that Margaret's suffering hadn't been prolonged. Others commented on the reality of her faith in Jesus Christ and how this had helped them. Each one reflected on Margaret's life and death, lost in personal sadness, not even sure others were listening to them. Suddenly one woman burst out angrily, "Why didn't God do something?"

The fog of grief suddenly cleared for me. Like Tolkien expressed in *The Return of the King,* I felt "like spring after winter, and sun on the leaves; and like trumpets and harps and all the songs I have ever heard." It was like an anthem of praise in my heart to be able to say, "He *has* done something."

God has done something about death. That's what the message of the Bible is all about. God has done something to redeem us from spiritual death and from physical death. It was not that I no longer felt sorrow at losing Margaret from my circle of friends. My missing her didn't change. It was simply that the fog had cleared. How awful if God had done nothing. How amazing that He has intervened out of personal concern for us. The Gospel is such Good News at a time like this.

How many times have we shouted out, "Why doesn't God do something?" And in our ignorance, our arrogance, and our frail humanity we have failed to grasp that He has acted in history and in our personal lives. We look only at partial data.

Death is a fact of life because sin is a fact of life. Death came because of sin (Romans 5:12). Both are the result of human choice. Spiritual death and physical death. Given a free will, the man and the woman chose to ignore their Creator, and in that decision they cut themselves off from free access to God. They experienced spiritual death.

> For although they knew God, they neither glorified him as God nor gave thanks to him, but their thinking became futile and their foolish hearts were darkened.

Romans 1:21

Cut off from God by personal choice. This is mankind—wretched, needing redemption, needing desperately to be brought back into the light of the One who in creation had said, "Let there be light," and there was light.

Sin brought its imbalance, its consequences to the whole world: thorns and thistles, the sweat of the brow, pain in childbirth (Genesis 3:16 ff.). The whole creation groans in travail, subject to the bondage of decay (Romans 8:21-22).

A pall of death hangs over life. Physical death is only part of this—a merciful part. Who would want to live while forever decaying? No, not that way, you say. But what of the infant or the one cut off in the fullness of youth? The mother, so necessary for the full nurture of her children? The father who is provider and lover? Sin is merciless in its rampage. Its strength is operative in the world. It is not rational; it is like a flooding stream.

Death and sin are not God's fault. His love wants us to

freely love in return, not respond as robots. And so He gave us a choice. He continues to let us choose. We have already discussed the torrent that entered the world at the first choice made. But evil and sadness do not take God by surprise. He is still sovereign. He is not a passive God who set the world running, like a giant clock, and then retired to His quiet chamber. The record of the Bible, and the experience of believing men and women, validate His personal concern. God *works* for the good of those who trust Him. He takes the yarn of our lives—the sadness and the gladness—and weaves into the warp and woof His own kind of blessing—a blessing which defies our normal concepts of happiness. And in His permissive will, He *allows* hard things to happen. In His mercy He *redeems* these hard experiences and builds strength into the lives of those who are disciplined by them.

Why does God allow death to strike down a father of three? He is not the author of evil. If He does not raise His hand to prevent the attack, then He asks us to look for a larger plan. He is the Creator, and He has evidenced His ability to create from our sorrows a psalm of praise.

In her book *His Thoughts Said . . . His Father Said,* Amy Carmichael captures our fearful thoughts about the future:

> But what of tomorrow? The Father speaks to those fears when he says: "Before trouble can meet thee it must pass through the brightness of My encompassing Presence, and passing through that brightness it loseth its darkness. It hath no more any power for evil. Also, as thou knowest well, I will be with thee in trouble." On this word the son stayed his heart, saying, "The Lord will take care of me. I will trust and not be afraid . . . ."

But we are digressing. What has God done about death? He has conquered it. He saw us ruined by our fall. We were unable to climb back to Him, and so, when time was ripe, He came to us. That's what the incarnation of Jesus Christ is all about. Who could conquer sin and death? Only God. And so He came in the person of Christ.

How did He come? As a baby. He entered the stream of human history to identify with us.

Why did He come? He said that He came to give His life as a ransom for many (Mark 10:45). He said He came to seek and to save those who are lost (Luke 19:10).

> . . . he also became a human being, so that by going through death as a man he might destroy him who had the power of death, that is, the devil; and might also set free those who lived their whole lives a prey to the fear of death.
>
> Hebrews 2:14-15 (Phillips)

> . . . he [Christ] has appeared once and for all to abolish sin by the sacrifice of Himself. And just as surely as it is appointed for all men to die once, and after that pass to their judgment, so it is certain that Christ was offered once to bear the sins of many and after that, to those who look for him, he will appear a second time, not this time to deal with sin, but to bring to full salvation those who eagerly await him.
>
> Hebrews 9:26-28 (Phillips)

John the Baptist pointed to Jesus and said, "Look, the Lamb of God, who takes away the sin of the world!" (John 1:29).

"I have come," said Jesus, "that they may have life, and have it to the full" (John 10:10).

"For what the law was powerless to do in that it was weakened by the sinful nature, God did by sending his own Son in the likeness of sinful man to be a sin offering. And so he condemned sin in sinful man . . . " (Romans 8:3).

God came as man to deal with our sin and with the penalty—death. That's why the angels proclaimed "good news of great joy" at the birth of Jesus. Good news. God has acted in history.

But that's not all. The resurrection of Jesus Christ from the dead validates the fact that God in Christ *has* defeated sin and death. Jesus Christ has "destroyed death and has brought life and immortality to light through the gospel" (2 Timothy 1:10). So wrote Paul just before he faced his own execution. How sweetly relevant this must have been to him.

The resurrection of Jesus Christ is supernatural; it is congruous with His claim to deity. If God is God, the resurrection is not a problem. And there is substantial historical evidence for this supernatural happening. The most convincing evidence is found in the lives of His disciples who proclaimed the news abroad that "the Lord has risen." The death of Christ had left them despondent, disillusioned. They had hoped for so much more. But death, that old enemy, had destroyed their hopes. Then their unbelief and sorrow were turned to joy. He was alive. In subsequent days they were prepared to hazard their very existence to preach that Christ arose from the dead, thus affirming His victory over sin and death.

It is this victory which is the theme of Paul's writing throughout the New Testament.

> But the truth is that Christ has been raised from death, as the guarantee that those who sleep in death will also be raised. For just as death came by means of a man, in the

same way the rising from death comes by means of a man. For just as all men die because of their union to Adam, in the same way all will be raised to life because of their union to Christ. But each one in his proper order: Christ, the first of all; then those who belong to Christ, at the time of his coming. Then the end will come; Christ will overcome all spiritual rulers, authorities, and powers, and hand over the Kingdom to God the Father. For Christ must rule until God defeats all enemies and puts them under his feet. The last enemy to be defeated will be death.

1 Corinthians 15:20-26 (TEV)

For we know that God, who raised the Lord Jesus to life, will also raise us up with Jesus and bring us, together with you, into his presence. All this is for your sake; and as God's grace reaches more and more people, they will offer more prayers of thanksgiving, to the glory of God.

For this reason we never become discouraged. Even though our physical being is gradually decaying, yet our spiritual being is renewed day after day. And this small and temporary trouble we suffer will bring us a tremendous and eternal glory, much greater than the trouble. For we fix our attention, not on things that are seen, but on things that are unseen. What can be seen lasts only for a time; but what cannot be seen lasts for ever.

For we know that when this tent we live in—our body here on earth—is torn down, God will have a house in heaven for us to live in, a home he himself made, which will last for ever. And now we sigh, so great is our desire to have our home which is in heaven put on over us; for by being clothed with it we shall not be found without a body. While we live in this earthly tent we groan with a feeling of oppression; it is not that we want to get rid of our earthly body, but that we want to have the heavenly one put on

over us, so that what is mortal will be swallowed up by life.
God is the one who has prepared us for this change, and he
gave us his Spirit as the guarantee of all that he has for us.

2 Corinthians 4:14-5:5 (TEV)

This is death in perspective, death transformed by the
resurrection of Jesus Christ as part of God's great plan of
redemption.

Death is unnatural. The separation of the spirit of a man
from his body—that's death. And it is wrong and sad. I
believe that is the reason why Jesus cried at Lazarus's tomb.
He knew He was going to raise Lazarus from the dead and
restore him to his family for at least a few more years. Yet He
stood at the tomb and wept—wept over sin's power to break
up families, over the cost of sin, over the corruption of sin.
But He also stood there and said, "I am the resurrection and
the life. He who believes in me will live, even though he dies;
and whoever lives and believes in me will never die" (John
11:25-26).

God values both body and spirit. When a person dies his
spirit goes to be with God. Away from the body and at home
with the Lord (2 Corinthians 5:8). Spiritually, a believer in
Christ has eternal life now by virtue of his personal faith in
Christ. Jesus said, "I tell you the truth, whoever hears my
word and believes him who sent me *has* eternal life and will
not be condemned; he *has crossed over* from death to life"
(John 5:24; italics mine).

Personal faith completes a spiritual transaction. Eternal
life is a present possession for believers. Death strikes. The
spirit goes to God; the body awaits a future redemption.

The body is important to God. What a man does with
his body matters in God's sight. When I talk with my

husband, I suppose it could be said that I am not talking to his body, but with his intellect and with his spirit. Yet I know him dressed in a body—a total person. The awful shock of death is that the body is there, but it is empty of the person who lived there. It's like a house that no longer is a home. Form without substance.

The beauty of the good news of God's redemption is that it includes our bodies. God has always cared about the *whole* person. He redeems us spiritually so that we can be alive forever in His fellowship. He also redeems our bodies. It is a consistent theme in the Scriptures; the resurrection of the body. For example,

> And if the Spirit of him who raised Jesus from the dead is living in you, he who raised Christ from the dead will also give life to your mortal bodies . . . .

Romans 8:11

> By his power God raised the Lord from the dead, and he will raise us also.

1 Corinthians 6:14

For a glorious doxology on the resurrection of the body, read Paul's words in 1 Corinthians 15:35-58, in which he answers the question, "How can the dead be raised to life? What kind of body will they have?" He compares mortality and immortality with corruptible and incorruptible. He says it is buried a physical body; when raised, it will be a spiritual body.

> Listen, I tell you a mystery: We will not all sleep, but we will all be changed—in a flash, in the twinkling of an eye, at the last trumpet. For the trumpet will sound, the dead

will be raised imperishable, and we will be changed . . .
then the saying that is written will come true: "Death has
been swallowed up in victory."

"Where, O death, is your victory?
Where, O death, is your sting?"

1 Corinthians 15:51-55

What happens to those who are still alive when Christ
reappears? They will be given a new body, as will those whose
bodies have decayed, been burned, eaten by sharks—or
destroyed in any other way. The perishable must be made
imperishable—and death's power is broken. Read
1 Thessalonians 4:13-18 for further insights into the glory of
that triumphant occasion.

Just as Christ appeared after His resurrection with a body
not subject to the normal laws of human flesh, so we will be
clothed in a resurrected, immortal body throughout eternity.

This is God's plan of redemption, and it is bigger than
present organic life. All of it is labeled *grace*. He did it all,
and it is not based on our achievements or good works. The
proof of God's amazing love is this: that it was *while we were
sinners* that Christ died for us (Romans 5:8). God has done
something about mankind's basic problems. What He has
done involves:

• the holiness of God
• the sinfulness of man
• the sacrifice of Jesus Christ to redeem us from sin and
death
• eternal life for all who believe.

Before the Gospel can be good news to anyone, it is first
of all bad news. God says we can't make it on our own, that

our moral failures (whether great or small) don't measure up to His standard of righteousness. He says we need redemption. And that's the moment of truth. Some people don't want to be redeemed: "Please, God, I'd rather do it myself." Which is a pretty drastic position to take when death waits at the door.

Redemption is accomplished and is awaiting the final day of completion. Participation in it is a personal matter. Heaven isn't for those who feel ill at ease with God. They wouldn't be happy there. The invitation is open to everyone to believe—to believe in a way that means handing over the reins of your life to a sovereign God.

God has done something about life and something about death. Trusting God is more than having someone to help you "cross over Jordan." It's getting in on the Triumph of the King, and understanding in fresh perspective what life is really all about. It means coming to our true home.

> The strife is o'er, the battle done;
> The victory of life is won;
> The song of Triumph has begun.
> Alleluia!

DELIVERANCE

Deliverance belongs to the Lord.

Psalm 3 (RSV)

TODAY in our family Bible reading we read the story of Jesus raising Lazarus from the dead and reuniting him with his sisters. Mark had amazing interest in this story for a six-year-old. He was quiet for a minute and then asked, "If Jesus could make Lazarus alive again, how come He let His dear friend John the Baptist stay dead after that wicked woman had him killed?"

On the surface it did seem unfair. One had a cruel death and the other was given life. That's how it looked to our Mark. That is how life's situations often look to me, too. God acted in one case; He did nothing in the other.

We talked about it for a while. Keith asked, "What happened to John the Baptist after he died? What happened to Lazarus after he was raised from the dead?" Lazarus was such a sensation that later he was almost the victim of a murder plot at the hand of angry religious leaders! And eventually he had to die again. Did God really deliver one and not the other—or is deliverance sometimes life and sometimes death?

I think Mark understood some of what we were talking about, at least as much as a small boy can.

(from my journal)

— • —

The subject of God's fairness in the way he delivers people came up again a year later when we were reading the book of Acts. Herod, in a fury, attacked the early church. Stirring events are covered with an economy of words:

> It was about this time that King Herod arrested some who belonged to the church, intending to persecute them. He had James, the brother of John, put to death with the sword. When he saw that this pleased the Jews, he proceeded to seize Peter also . . . . After arresting him, he put him in prison, handing him over to be guarded by four squads of four soldiers each. Herod intended to bring him out for public trial after the Passover.
>
> So Peter was kept in prison, but the church was earnestly praying to God for him.
>
> The night before Herod was to bring him to trial, Peter was sleeping between two soldiers, bound with two chains, and sentries stood guard at the entrance. Suddenly an angel of the Lord appeared and a light shone in the cell. He struck Peter on the side and woke him up. "Quick, get up!" he said, and the chains fell off Peter's wrists.

Acts 12:1-7

Furthermore, Peter dressed, put on his shoes, wrapped himself in his cloak, and walked out past the guards; the iron gate opened by itself.

Peter's deliverance is an exciting story—and it looks like God went to some work to accomplish it. Chains, guards, iron gates of prison—even a man to get dressed and out on the street. But poor James. He got nothing. No deliverance. And his escape looked like such a simple thing for God to accomplish. Just have the soldier miss with his sword, trip over a rock, fall off his horse—anything would have seemed simpler than freeing a chained man in prison.

Have you ever felt like that—that maybe God didn't know what He was doing? Good people, such dear little children, a beloved wife—these die while the wicked and ordinary go on living. Or maybe you've tried harder to do right than most other people, and your child is the one who is killed on the street of your hometown. Your husband is gunned down, caught in senseless violence. What of this? It seems unfair.

Was Peter delivered and James not? James went to be with Jesus Christ, the One whom he had loved and served. He was delivered. Delivered from further persecution, delivered from the confusion that followed the persecution. He was delivered in an ultimate sense. Peter's deliverance seems more real to us, but only because we are so earthbound. God delivers His children. It is not our prerogative to tell Him the best way to do it. And this is good, because we often have foggy vision in the matter of deliverance.

Part of our problem is an inadequate comprehension of what heaven is like. Heaven is being with the King of all the universe, the Creator, having fellowship with Him and enjoying life without the impediments of sin, weakness and insecurity. We've never known such freedom and have difficulty conceiving of it. Reading the last two chapters of Revelation regularly would freshen our heavenly senses.

God understands our failings in this area. He made us to delight in what He created on earth. There is a holy exultation in life that is pleasing to God. We rejoice in the magnificence of creation; we sing with the psalmist of the mercies of the Lord. Life is sweet. He means it to be even sweeter than it is. The goodness of earth is only a shadow, a foretaste of what is to come.

The neighbor boy who was staying overnight at our home listened to the Bible story we read. Somehow heaven came into the conversation, and he decided he didn't want to go there. I asked why. He said, "Who wants to just sit around all day with a harp?" Not too many people do. I wondered if he thought of heaven as being confined to wearing pajamas or bathrobes forever! We need to begin to wonder at what the Creator might have beyond this life for His own children to enjoy. Given all the marvels of earth, what will heaven be? The Bible speaks of reigning with Christ, of being joint-heirs, of sharing His glory. What an exhilarating future!

In his marvelous allegory, *The Last Battle*, C. S. Lewis stirs the imagination in his descriptions of Aslan's country, "where everything is more real—as different as a real thing is from a shadow or as wakening life is from a dream."

> The new [country] was a deeper country: every rock and flower and blade of grass looked as if it meant more. I can't describe it any better than that: if you ever get there, you will know what I mean.
>
> It was the Unicorn who summed up what everyone was feeling. He stamped his right fore-hoof on the ground and neighed and then cried:

"I have come home at last! This is my real country! I belong here. This is the land I have been looking for all my life, though I never knew it till now. The reason why we loved the old Narnia is that it sometimes looked a little like this . . . . Come further up, come further in!" . . .

"The further up and the further in you go, the bigger everything gets. The inside is larger than the outside." . . . and Aslan is there.

"Now at last they were beginning Chapter One of the Great Story, which no one on earth has read: which goes on for ever: in which every chapter is better than the one before," writes Lewis at the conclusion of the book. We ought to sigh a little when we think of heaven.

The question of God's deliverance comes up and most often in the area of severe illness. Sometimes it is not a matter of life or death, but a matter of suffering or deformity. Occasionally one hears a minister or a healer who says, "It is not God's will that any of you enjoy less than perfect health. If you really believe, you can be healed."

We do read of many whom Jesus healed, and of others healed by His disciples. However, there is no record that He healed everyone. Many must have been unable to get to Him. If healing was of prime importance, would not Jesus have compassionately sought these out? And what of Paul, who said that he pleaded with the Lord three times to take away his "thorn in the flesh" and God's answer was, "My grace is sufficient for you, for my power is made perfect in weakness"? Was Paul's faith too weak?

God does heal by removing actual physical problems. He is still the Great Physician, yet most of us think more quickly of seeing the medical doctor at the clinic than we do of talking things over with Him. But God also heals in ways

that we do not ask. He offers His sufficient grace, the beauty
of His character caught in the prism of life.

A "terminal illness" presents a more severe trial to faith.
And more severe confusion ensues. Is the medic who says
"terminal" omniscient? Should we pray for healing? Can we
be sure of God's will before we pray, so that we ask in full
faith, not having to add "if it be Your will"? Is much prayer
the secret, or much faith? Whole books have been written on
the subject of faith healing, and you may want to read some
of them. It's a sensitive area. Only be aware of one danger.
Do not box God up into your concept of deliverance. He
will be God, the Deliverer. And He will deliver—some into a
larger life on earth, others through much pain with joy, and
many into the glory of His presence.

Letting God be the Deliverer means trusting His
character in a basic way. It means believing He is God. It's a
lifetime exercise.

I tried to deliver a friend once. That is, I wanted to stand
between the awful hurt of death and my friend, as if I could
protect her. One of our closest friends was drowned while
canoeing at our campsite. He didn't return from his short
trip out into the bay. His wife and children were on the way
up to join us for the weekend. The waiting was a nightmare.
All night long I pleaded with God to deliver Paul, to let him
be found on some island or downshore, lost but alive. I
objected when my husband contacted his wife to warn her of
our fears for his life. The search parties looked long into the
night and were actually in more danger than the original
canoe trip involved. But day came, and with it the reality of
death.

What do you say to one of your dearest friends? How do
you tell her that her husband, father of three, is dead? I
wanted to soften the truth, to avoid it, to do anything to save

the hurt. I have never wanted so much to be bigger than life. My husband finally helped me. He said, "Don't stand between. You can't deliver her; only God can."

She already knew when she arrived that he was drowned. And I watched God deliver a widow in her grief. He filled her mind and her mouth with His truth and His perspective. He gave her grace to see beyond this life, through all her sorrow. It wasn't what I would ever have planned to demonstrate the glory of God. But it was life—cold, hard life—lived out in the reality of the grace of God. He delivered and He kept on delivering. And He will deliver. It isn't an easy road. But He is there, and that makes all the difference.

Deliverance involves believing that God's will and His love are the same thing.

> The righteous cry out, and the LORD hears them; he delivers them from all their troubles. The LORD is close to the brokenhearted and saves those who are crushed in spirit.

> I sought the LORD, and he answered me; he delivered me from all my fears.

> Psalm 34:17-18, 4

FEARS

MARK AND MARIAN came into town today to see Dick at the hospital. He greeted them with, "Well, have you come to see me before I die?" It certainly unmasked reality.

When we went to see him later today I heard him tell the nurse that she was keeping him out of heaven with all her medical procedures. He seems to have accepted the fact that his time is limited. Or is it bravado? What does he think about when he wakens in the night? Still, I think he is less afraid than most people.

(from my journal)

—•—

*G*ood theology is the secret to both living and dying. Theology isn't heavy and dull, as some imagine. Good theology simply means having the facts straight. It is not our ideas that matter; it is God's truth that is crucial. To die according to truth is as important as living according to truth. That is why reviewing the basics sharpens the perspective and refreshes the heart. Otherwise we are led by fears and plagued by misunderstandings.

Someone once said that the statistics about death are pretty impressive: one out of one dies. That may be a tongue-in-cheek remark, but in reality death comes to all of us. It isn't a question of if, but when. Yet we postpone thinking about death until we are stopped short by a severe illness or the malfunctioning of our bodies.

Facing your own mortality is a large experience. Helping someone you love face theirs may be an even larger experience. How do you help someone you love die? We want to shout death away and we pray earnestly for miracles. No other experience tests our humanity so much or makes us more aware of how frail and vulnerable we are.

"The tumor is malignant. We could not remove all of it. He has about six months." What a devastating blow words like these bring to the person with the tumor. But those words are also shattering to everyone close to that person—family, friends, the church, even the medical people who say them. Everyone who cares feels an incredible stress; the closer the relationship, the greater the gloom and tension. It is too frightening; our thoughts blur; we can't think of anything to say. Both the living and the dying are caught in the event. A rush of fear and overwhelming helplessness make people want to hide from each other. What can anyone say?

In her study, *On Death and Dying*, Dr. Elisabeth Kubler-Ross describes five stages of feeling common in the lives of dying patients. I believe those closest to the terminally ill experience the same feelings. The immediate reaction is to deny death. It's too much to face. It's hard to even grasp the information. Many patients and their family members remember only part of the diagnosis and because it is so frightening, they rearrange the data with selective listening.

Coping is hard. Denial gives some space for facing reality. The patient may talk freely about the prognosis with one person and deny the problem with another, often the one closest to him. Both may feel that the tests were misread, say they want to check with another doctor, or in other ways say that it can't be true.

It is not particularly helpful to say, "You're not facing the truth!" to someone who is having trouble coping. It's better to respond with sympathy and understanding for the feelings the person expresses. Being both heard and understood are so important. Often in the expression of denial, reality comes into focus.

Some, quicker to face reality, skip the denial and react immediately with anger. Why me? What have I done wrong? Family members may be angry and bitter at the overwhelming unfairness of having their own taken in this way. They may envy others whose lives seem so untouched and lash out against the world.

Cutting remarks or harsh accusations are a way of striking back at an unsafe world, but these only make the lonely reality more painful. We need to understand what is happening inside ourselves and the other person. Accepting anger as a legitimate emotion and talking it through leads to some solution. Christians often don't know how to handle anger because it isn't on the list of approved emotions. We have deceived ourselves in facing reality. Admitting honest feeling is part of the inner healing process. The psalmists did it repeatedly with words like these:

When I was in distress, I sought the Lord . . .
and my soul refused to be comforted.

Psalm 77:2

My heart is in anguish within me;
the terrors of death assail me.

Fear and trembling have beset me;
horror has overwhelmed me.

Psalm 55:4, 5

I pour out my complaint before him;
before him I tell my trouble.
When my spirit grows faint within me,
it is you who know my way.

Psalm 142:2-3

God is bigger than our anger. He can cut through with
His peace in His time. We all need friends who are
sympathetic to our feelings, who love and pray us through
our distresses. Both the sick person and the family need this
kind of support.

Eventually we must face the inevitable. Some may
struggle for the short space of an afternoon or two days;
others may take weeks or months. The time span is not as
important as feeling loved and understood during the
struggle. It is too lonely to face alone.

A time of bargaining may follow. "If I can just live to see
Lisa married." "We had planned this event for so long. If
Edward can just be well enough . . . ." Times of depression
come and go as new surges of hope rise and wane. A friend,
torn by the depression her husband was experiencing as he
went in for chemotherapy, said his conversation had been full
of frustration and "if only." "But God must have met him on
the way," she said. "Quite unexpectedly his attitude changed.
He seemed so free." A few days later he was again depressed
and so was his wife. Emotional ups and downs are exhausting.

What can one do to help? Allow the honest expression of
sorrow or defeat. Give loving support and concern as well as

comfort. And pray. Companionship and understanding tears are more important than words.

The final stage in Kubler-Ross's study is acceptance. The fight against the inevitable ends. I may not get well. I am dying. Both the patient and the loved one may experience a sense of withdrawal. The patient, especially, may seem harder to talk to and live increasingly within his own thoughts. At this time it becomes even more important to continue expressing care and affirming worth, even though the person may seem remote.

Some have programmed the Kubler-Ross stages into the experience of every terminally ill person. I object to boxing people in that way. Be careful not to go around looking for or insisting on stages of feelings—or to recite them to those who are ill. The value of understanding these stages is to help those who are suffering to react with compassion for themselves and others. Especially if someone is quiet or on the edge of the experience (as a child might be), don't assume they are not experiencing the denial and rage that the threat of death brings.

The dying person needs assurance that his feelings and his rights will be taken seriously. And the patient does have rights. One of the most frightening aspects of illness is losing control over one's life. Decisions are made about your body and its treatment almost without permission. Others take over details you have always cared for yourself. You can be wheeled in and out or poked with needles with no explanation. Medical treatment can make a person feel like a thing. The patient has the right to full information and, knowing the options, has the right to refuse treatment.

The basic rights of respectful, considerate care, privacy and confidentiality are important. Well-meaning people seem to talk down to sick people. The family needs to be on guard against the humiliation of the loss of personal dignity and the depersonalization that dependency often brings to the ill.

Whenever possible, ask the advice of the ill person about some detail of family care or decision-making. This reinforces the importance of his contribution to life. Sometimes families strip away all responsibilities and decisions, thinking to save the sick from details and worries. This isolation from the mainstream of life can make the person feel worthless and as good as dead.

Losing control over one's life is only one fear the seriously ill face. *What if I become totally helpless and dependent? What if I can't stand the pain? What if my behavior is irresponsible?* All kinds of fears lurk in the mind, especially in the middle of the night. No one wants to be incompetent about the basics of life.

Being God's person in helping the terminally ill individual is a great responsibility. If that person is an integral part of your own existence the privilege and pain increase with the degree of intimacy you have enjoyed. What can you do?

First of all, be a good listener. Don't worry so much about what to say. Give your full attention to the other person's needs. Really hear what he is saying and even what he is not saying.

That is easier said than done. Coping with your own hurts can divide your attention. You have an agenda operating in your own head and heart. That agenda needs to be handled, too, perhaps with someone else outside the family, so that you can get your own thoughts clarified.

Where did we get the idea that we need an answer to every dimension of human need? *What will I say?* keeps people worrying instead of ministering. Having someone listen with the heart and take you seriously is one of life's most satisfying encounters. What to say will come from *really* listening.

Secondly, be sensitive. There aren't any easy answers so don't try to give any. Scripture verses may not offer the comfort you intend, unless they are given with a good deal of empathy. Some people, including ministers, want to slap Romans 8:28 onto a hurt and thus dissolve the pain. It doesn't work. We know that in everything God works for good with those who love him, who are called according to his purpose. Romans 8:28 is great truth, but it isn't a band-aid for every situation. Don't use Scripture as your only communication with a person.

Sick people feel isolated by the experience. It's like being in another world. The side effects of drugs and pain may increase isolation. Your presence, your touch, your familiar voice, your warmth of relationship—what a relief, even if it seems unappreciated. It means I am not alone. Touching says much more than many words, important as words are. All the way through life—young, old, middle age—touching is the special language of caring.

Love must be expressed with words, too. It is very difficult for some people to say what is in the heart. Say it now. Don't wish you had said it sometime later. When my brother phoned me to say that our Dad had died, we couldn't talk for a while, overwhelmed with loss. Then he said, "We wouldn't have done anything differently, would we? He knew we loved him, and we knew he loved us." I can't tell you what a balm that was to our hearts, to our whole family. No missed communication. Talk while you have each other.

One other thing you can do: offer hope. Not false hope, not lies, but something tangible. The hope of recovery is not the only hope you can offer. The hope of seeing the children tomorrow afternoon at 3 p.m. The hope of going home for the weekend. The hope of solving an inconvenience, a pain or distress. An encouraging gift. An unexpected visit. A piece of news or a bright spot to focus on. Some goodness that you appreciate together. We cannot live without hope. That is why the Gospel is such good news at a time like this. Heaven is real; it is our sure hope.

Stress what is positive. But at the same time, be honest. Nothing is phonier than false brightness. We don't need to avoid uncomfortable subjects when God's grace is available to us. Empathize. What needs to be done? What desires need to be cared for? What unspoken needs can be met that will make a brighter tomorrow? Even a favorite thing to eat can make a difference.

Hope inevitably brings up the question of miraculous healing. How do you help someone facing death to handle this subject? On the one hand, not to consider that God might heal is to say that He is powerless in the face of medical opinion. That kind of hopelessness would scarcely benefit you or the dying one.

On the other hand, terminally ill people can be exploited by positive statements about healing made by well-meaning people. When one mother called a public prayer number to ask for healing, she got the word, "Your daughter will be healed. Only believe." Her daughter was not healed. Did she fail to believe enough? Just when a person needs a strong assurance of God's love, doubt is cast about their belief and about God's care. Catherine Marshall wisely writes from her own experience about the importance of knowing the difference between "presumption that masquerades as faith and real faith." God is not obliged to prove anything to any of us.

Then how should the subject of healing be handled? With faith that God is able to do whatever He wishes done.

We ask, in faith, for His will. He can heal; He has done it. He may choose to intervene in a different way. God is always intervening in our lives; His intervention may be release in death. Real faith trusts His character and lets Him decide what is best. The spiritual exercise of casting our whole being on God always makes His love more real.

Diets and certain natural foods are often urged on those judged terminally ill. Usually someone has a miracle story to tell and people choose up sides about the value of the theory. It's important to keep our faith in the living God, not in either foods or medicine. However, since all medical data is not complete, an individual should be allowed the freedom of trying whatever sounds hopeful. Its value may be chiefly in the hope and be neither helpful nor hurtful. Just the "doing something" may relieve anxiety and thus be constructive.

Finally, the best help we can offer is our spiritual support. In a sense, it is our privilege to trust God for those who may be feebly reaching toward Him in the confusion of illness. We can pray. We can share God's Word.

One of my friends, a young mother of thirty-four, heard news of the recurrence of cancer cells. She was told her time was limited. I went to see Mary Lynne one day and brought her what I knew she was prepared to receive: cookies for her children and a ribbon of Bible promises, to be opened one at a time as they were needed. We put the cookies on the kitchen table and hung the promise ribbon on the kitchen wall. We cried together and I told her that I had no answers, but on that ribbon were things I knew to be true about God. She knew I loved her, that I was scared with her.

I would have had difficulty getting through a prayer with her that day, but as the weeks went by we were drawn closer and closer by what she was discovering as she opened promise after promise from the ribbon. She ministered to me with the truths from God's Word that I had prepared for her. The whole church was blessed by her practical claiming of these promises. Somehow God enabled her to share what was happening inside her with the people she talked with, in prayer meetings and whenever it seemed appropriate to her. She became surer of God's mercy as others became more concerned about her condition.

Mary Lynne had always questioned God and why he did what he did. In every Bible study group she belonged to she seemed to have an objection to God's methods. Now she began believing every promise she came across and trusting him in ways we never saw before. She moved from being a doubter of God's goodness to a communicator of His utter reliability. And she did this as she faced death and having to leave her husband and two small daughters. She grabbed hold of truth and made it real in her life. Her faith was infectious.

At about four o'clock in the morning on which she died, John, a concerned young man in our church family, awakened and thought about Mary Lynne. He felt compelled to go to the hospital. Fran, a member of the church family who was on duty caring for her, told John that she thought the end might be near. Mary Lynne seemed comatose. John began reading aloud from the last of Revelation. At the description of heaven, Mary Lynne suddenly sat up, opened her eyes and seemed to want to say something. She listened for a moment. Then she lay back on her pillow and entered heaven herself.

She involved many of us in her dying, and all of us love God more for the experience. Being human means entering into relationships that allow us to share our fears, our hope, our faith, our dying and our living—and in doing so to feel God's love poured into our hearts.

Even though I walk through the valley of the
shadow of death,

I will fear no evil, for you are with me . . . .

Psalm 23:4

GRIEF

O LORD, I WEEP for my sister. So different from me, yet so like me. All earthly relationships now finished since you have torn her away from us who loved her, who counted on her being there. She was the initiator of family gatherings and family gifts to others, the stable one, the one who was there—at home. You could phone and she would answer. The one who kept the people connections straight, who stayed in touch with childhood friends. I thought she would grow old like mother and hold our family together as we faced our later years . . . . She grew more beautiful as she grew older. The fruit of the Spirit worked out in her. My brother said she gave herself for others, and as he said it, the overwhelming truth of it seemed to define her life.

O Lord, the terrible pain of all of us hearing, disbelieving, facing the hard reality of her loss, a broken circle. We have a new vulnerability—my brothers and I. Our family is only immortal as it hides in You, Lord. Heal us, O Lord. We wait for your comfort . . . .

(from my journal)

— • —

*G*rief is a smothery feeling. She is dead. It is a hard sentence to learn to live with.

"No one ever told me that grief felt so like fear. I am not afraid, but the sensation is like being afraid. The same fluttering in the stomach, the same restlessness, the yawning. I keep on swallowing." So wrote C. S. Lewis after the death of his wife in *A Grief Observed.*

It is like suspense. Like waiting for what isn't going to happen. A suspension in time. Does what happens next even matter? It is like loosing a mooring point and being at sea—way out, where even familiar landmarks blur.

Mark Twain's daughter Susy died suddenly at the age of twenty-four. Writing about this in his autobiography, Twain helps us understand something of the impact of sudden death. He writes

> It is one of the mysteries of our nature that a man, all unprepared, can receive a thunder-stroke like that and live. There is but one reasonable explanation of it. The intellect is stunned by the shock and but gropingly gathers the meaning of the words. The power to realize their full impact is mercifully wanting. The mind has a dumb sense of vast loss—that is all. It will take mind and memory months and possibly years to gather the details and thus learn and know the whole extent of the loss.

That is why grief is such a long process. We cannot comprehend the loss all at once. It is emotional overload and takes some getting used to. Grieving makes us sigh a lot. Something terrible is wrong and we can't grasp its significance all in one thought.

The hot prick of an unexpected memory can tumble joy and grief into rivers of feeling that leave one blubbering like a child. Then the river dries up. And what follows is a sensation of drowning in a life that is flat, dull and barren.

One woman said she found herself craving soft foods and sleeping a lot. Her concentration went awry; it was hard to read. She wanted to talk with people about what was happening to her, but felt embarrassed to keep bringing up her pain, as if she expected her feelings to be the center of everyone else's universe. And then there are the children; how does one meet their needs when you can't even meet your own? Grief is exhausting.

"Give sorrow words," Shakespeare said in *Macbeth*. "The grief that does not speak whispers the o'er-fraught heart, and bids it break." That's good advice. People who bottle up their grief pay for it in other ways, often with serious physical problems or a bitter spirit. Complaining, sharing problems, talking about the deceased and unabashed weeping ventilate an over-taxed system.

Sorrow is a valid emotion. It should not embarrass us, nor make us feel weak. Grief is like a journey one must take on a winding mountainside, often seeing the same scenery many times, a road which eventually leads to somewhere we've never been before.

God does not hand out medals to those who do not weep. Weeping is normal; it is abnormal to pretend there is no sorrow. He made us with a capacity to feel. Remember that Jesus wept.

Grief is an immensely personal thing. It is too big to carry alone, yet no one else can really help. Except God. But is He there? Even heaven may seem hard and brassy. Some want to yell out at Him about the injustice of what He has allowed. Others say all the right things—He's in a better place; she is with the Lord; who knows what God has saved him from? But they sound like clanging lies. We want to shout aloud how much he had to live for, about her capacity to live life as it ought to be lived, about the special kind of happiness he knew.

God understands about grief. The Son of Man is "a man of sorrows and acquainted with grief." If we understand anything at all about the cross we know God understands suffering. Our grief, our confusion, our doubts, our anger are safe with Him. We can tell Him all of these—in sobs or in shouts—and He will hear us. We may have to wait to hear and see Him in return. We can't hear when we're screaming and we can't see properly when our eyes are blurred with tears. But He will wait. We determine our capacity to receive from God, but even here He uses time to heal our exhaustion, and tenderness to heal our aches until we want Him.

We think of the one we lost. We think too much and with too much grief, and instead of the person becoming more real in our memory, the loved one becomes more and more a creation of our own mind, not the person he really was. Passionate grief does not link us with the dead, but cuts us off from them. That's the problem with too many visits to the grave, keeping his room as it was, setting her place at the table—or whatever sentimental tricks we use to try to deny change. We only make the loved one seem more dead.

It's very easy to feel sorry for yourself. My dear friend who just lost her husband tells me how vulnerable she feels. When something goes wrong, she feels almost too fragile to handle the situation, and yet she must. It doesn't seem fair, but much of life isn't fair. She keeps waiting for what will happen next. Everything seems so perplexing and this makes her feel incompetent, like she can't think straight. She knows all the right answers but she can't control these feelings that make her want to crawl in a hole somewhere and hide until it all goes away. Sometimes when people are the kindest she responds by being the weepiest. Her emotions keep playing tricks on her.

Sometimes as a last priority, our thoughts turn to God. Ourselves, our loved one, God. That's the imbalance of grief. Life only makes sense when we reverse the order. Feelings push God out of place. It's natural to feel despair, but when it goes on too long and the focus is always on me, then I have reached a dead-end street. God is the great illuminator; he is the one who assures that "your light will rise in the darkness, and your night will become like the noonday." Still it is easier to talk about than to realize in the middle of the disorientation that grief brings. We have to be patient with ourselves and with each other in the struggle to regain our equilibrium.

Sorrow can mix up our priorities. We become absorbed with ourselves in a selfish way, although we don't want to be told this. We meet others who sorrow, but we are sure their grief is not the same as ours. It isn't; it is their grief, not ours. And who is to say whether it hurts more to lose a wife or a husband, a child or a parent, a brother or a sister? Our own sorrow is always worse.

Some sorrows are worse than others because they demand that we work through tender relationships while we are seriously wounded. Suicide brings a terrible pain and unending questions. Was I insensitive? What could I have done? Didn't I hear what she was saying? Guilt. And rejection. Did he think so little of us that he would do this? How could she do this to me? The rejection is almost worse than the death. Who can describe this kind of pain?

The death of a child can bring a stress to marriage that surprises many. One would think that because they are together in grief, a husband and wife could comfort each other. And often they can and do. But grief is a private thing and people express it differently. Sometimes our grieving doesn't match in kind. A wife can resent her husband for seeming happiness when she feels so devastated. A husband can wonder how much his wife really cares if she could be so interested in mundane things. One may want to talk about the loss; the other may want to steer conversation away from the sadness. With all the best intentions, people can miss each other in the ways they communicate grief.

When a couple has lost a child they have borne together they need help in communicating and understanding each other. A very high percentage of marriages dissolve because two people grow apart during the grieving period. Taking time to work through grief—not as an emotion to be done away with but as a process to profit from—can enrich even desperately saddened lives.

When death hits us we are forced to try the rope. All the things we have said we believed—will they hold now? For some it is a struggle; for others it is easier to view life from God's perspective. Not without tears in either case, not without the journey of grief. But with a Companion on the journey. I am inclined to believe that special resources are made available to us when we need them, but that our capacity to receive from God and others is determined by the integrity of our relationship to God beforehand. A person who has been regularly drinking at the fountain of living water knows where to go when he is parched and dry. Another, used to digging his own well, may struggle to find the path to the Fountain.

People get over the pain of sorrow. Time is a great healer. Both of these facts are blessings. Still grief dies hard for most people and comes bubbling back up through the years. Perhaps it is easier to experience God's comfort to our spiritual nature, but it is harder to comfort the motherhood, the lover, the child in us that has lost its entire being through death.

For instance, I find it hard to accept emotionally the fact that one day I will lose my mother as I have lost my father, unless the Lord returns first. She will have a joyful entrance into the presence of God, having loved and trusted Him for many years. My reluctance to let her go does not mean that I begrudge her heaven's comforts. But something about her being here makes family closer. When she leaves I will no longer be anyone's child, a privilege I now enjoy even though I am a grown woman. And what of no longer being a wife, a husband, a mother or a father! The sorrow is twofold: missing the person and missing the joy of the relationship.

Grief makes us lazy. We don't plan, for there seems less to plan for. That is why widows become careless in how they look, and widowers fail to plan proper meals. A bereaved mother may even neglect her other children and husband, seeming to think more of what was lost than what can still be enjoyed. Or we put up a curtain between ourselves and the world. We shut ourselves off, even from people we love most. Grief scares us and makes us feel things we cannot put into words, and so we box ourselves away from those who want to intrude. A father, losing a favorite son, can also effectively lose his wife and other children in this way.

We need desperately at times like these to turn to the Creator, the Prime Mover in life, and let Him move and motivate us. He can tear down barriers we have built up; He can open us up; He can show us a creative way to use our sorrow. He gives us a future. God wants us to say "yes" to life. Sorrow teaches and deepens us in ways that joy does not. Recently a woman who had lost a child remarked that many of her previous acquaintances seemed surprisingly shallow. It was not they who had changed; she had changed. Sorrow is strangely enriching.

The world is full of people who need love and understanding. The wise and creative person eventually looks away from a past which cannot be altered and finds a way to do some of the loving and understanding. The returns are always greater than the investment. No widow need eat alone night after night when there are other widows who are also eating alone. No mother need leave her arms empty, or long for a teenager to eat her chocolate cake, if she wants to reach outside of herself into the lives of others.

I remember reading of a widow who, on her deceased husband's birthday, celebrated the day by baking a cake and taking it to a busy mother with small children. A visit to the hospital, loaning a book you've enjoyed, showing hospitality—there are a thousand ways to send out feelers into the mainstream of life.

People who stand still in life, closed up tight against whatever God might offer, never learn how to let anything important happen to them. Time just runs itself out. It takes courage to put first things first, to risk new adventure, to rearrange existence, even if it means burning bridges best left behind. The adventure of life is not finished. In God's plan for us there is always something new, something exciting and wonderful, no matter what our age. The past is always an apprenticeship for a new adventure, a new rhythm. Yes, even in old age when the final adventure will be death itself. The greatest adventure of all is to know God in new dimensions of life.

A friend of mine gave me this insightful reminder which I now keep in my notebook:

We are apt to forget that our Heavenly Guide and an earthly guide have different purposes. The one studies to give us an uneventful safe journey; God is interested in the qualities we develop on the journey, not the safeness and softness of the trip.

We expect to be guided wide of every danger and He leads us over mountains and into impossible corners through deep waters of trouble and gets us to Heaven all breathless with excitement and exertion; but fitted for royal fellowship and capacitated for more joy unspeakable and full of glory.

Author Unknown

If you cannot bear thought of adventure with God right now, don't turn aside. If grief is more real to you than God, don't be afraid. Grief is not a short road for many. The way out is found in God, not in helpful suggestions about ways to live life. Hudson Taylor was led to pray a prayer you may want to make your own:

O Jesus make Thyself to me
A living bright Reality;
More real, more intimately nigh
Than even the sweetest earthly tie.

SYMPATHY

What sorrow was, thou badst her know,
And from her own she learn'd to melt at others' woe.

Thomas Gray in *Hymn to Adversity*

LAST NIGHT we received a call that D and J's baby had been born but would probably not live through the night because of serious deformities. Both of them were holding and loving the baby because the doctors think it is only a matter of hours. Our hearts nearly broke remembering their excitement over the pregnancy and all their dreams for this baby. What to do? Somehow we just had to go to the hospital to be there after it was all over. There wasn't anything we could do, but we had to let them know how much we cared that this had happened to them. Neither of them have any parents in this city and maybe we could take that role. We felt right about doing this, even though we may not be the people closest to them, and we were there to cry with them and to care . . . .

(from my journal)

— • —

Sympathy. How do you express to a person that you really care that death has taken away someone he loves? Thomas Gray was right. Those who do it best have learned what sorrow is and know genuine empathy.

One spring day a little boy in our neighborhood died from a rare disease. The news spread from house to house and women wept for the parents and for the loss of a dear two-year-old. Late in the afternoon men and women stood in groups in front of their houses, discussing the event while their own children played around them. Unexpectedly the parents of the dead boy drove into their driveway. No one had seen them since the news of the death. There was a momentary freezing of conversation and activity, and then neighbors grabbed their healthy, beautiful, alive children and disappeared into their houses. Only one couple did the natural thing—ran over to them in concern and simply said, "I'm so sorry," and wept a little.

Didn't the others care? Of course they did. But at that moment they felt almost apologetic for having children who were alive and they didn't know what to say. They were scared by what had happened. Scared and too paralyzed to act naturally.

The inability to be natural in the face of another's sorrow is added pain to the bereaved. In this case, the parents felt that they were an embarrassment to their neighbors, on top of all their personal grief.

It comes in other ways. The widow and the widower feel friends avoiding them or else sense their wondering, *Shall we mention it? What shall we say?* Or the married people who seem almost embarrassed about their happy union when another's has just been broken by death. At a time when grief is more than enough to cope with, we ought to act confidently and positively so that we do not add to the burden of the bereaved by our own inadequacy.

The other extreme, of course, is the babbler who says too much—who offers all the glib consolations that make a person want to shout out, "If you think it's that easy, you just don't understand." Job's comforters made long speeches about causes and cures for his sorrow. They had done better when they simply came and sat in sympathetic silence.

It can be awkward to be on the receiving end of sympathy. The bereaved needs his friends so much, but sometimes it is hard for him to take in what they are saying. The burden of relating well in this situation should be placed on the one offering sympathy, not on the bereaved. Comforted are those whose friends stay near, but make few demands on the sorrowing. Being a genuine friend in the hour of death is not easy.

What we want most in our sorrow is the comfort of knowing that others understand in even a small measure what our loss means to us. They care that we hurt inside, that we feel bewildered and lost. If we need their advice, we'll ask for it. Otherwise we just want their psychological and spiritual support. It isn't great speeches that comfort; it is feeling another's sympathy in our awful exposure to human frailty.

A pressed hand or an embrace, with a lumped-up throat that prohibits effective speech, the sympathy in your eyes, communicates better than a prepared speech. Tears are not outlawed. Your own most natural way to show that you understand and care is the best sympathy you can offer. If you are an emotional person with a compulsion to weep or go morbidly over the details, show your sympathy as constructively as you can, and then leave. If you are a

Christian, pray. It's the best help you can offer. But don't agonize over what to say; simply say, "I'm standing with you,"—or whatever simple expression is naturally your own. You are not there to explain death; you have come to say you care about the living or loved the one who died.

Don't say, "If there is anything I can do, let me know." A grieving person in a state of shock is hardly able to inform you about what needs doing. If you see something to do, do it. Volunteer specific help. Be as unobtrusive as possible during the immediate aftermath of death when life is confusing. Be sensitive to the conversational needs of the bereaved.

Comfort is a wonderful word. Take it apart and notice its Latin derivatives: com (*con*-Latin) means *with*; *forte* means *strength*. To comfort another is to come with strength. Sympathy can be comfort; but it is not always the same. Sympathy is a valid way to say, "We're brothers. I care that this happened to you." Comfort is the gift only a few will bring the bereaved. And they will bring it out of their personal inner resources.

A person who fears death does not usually bring comfort to the grieved. He can offer the support of one insecure person reaching out in sympathy to another. Do not think lightly of this. But comfort comes from those who have coped with the issues of life and death in their own souls and offer to the other the strength they have found.

It is easiest to offer comfort to believers, to those who know how to trust God even in small ways. Something binds people together who both fellowship with God. It's a family affair as you stand before God together, expecting His comfort and deliverance in the hard hours. It is two people coming to a capable God on behalf of one of them.

When death catches a person unprepared for mortality,

sympathy is offered, but comfort is strained. The dimension of hope is not there. I feel personal freedom to speak of praying that God will reach into life with His healing touch. Another's belief does not condition my belief. I cannot ultimately deliver any sorrowing person; I can entrust him to the God of all comfort. I can expose him to the comfort I have experienced. And I can be a friend.

Sympathy comes by the bushel immediately after death. And it's good that it does. Facing the shock of events alone would be difficult. But three weeks later, six weeks later, and even more, six months later—when the painful awareness of the loss sinks deeply into our beings—we need our friends more than ever. Most of the time all but a few have forgotten our sorrow.

That's the time for creative friendship. Suggest a definite plan: a luncheon, an invitation for golf and supper. A telephone call, especially at twilight or on the weekends, may rescue lonely hours. Share your family. A shopping trip, stopping by to offer a ride on a rainy day, an extra ticket for a concert or play are all ways to ease the recovery of someone who has suffered the loss of a loved one. If a person is not used to going places alone, even going to church alone can be a traumatic experience. Sharing your life and resources is what friendship is about, and it is a practical affair. Make the person feel needed and wanted because of who he is.

In coping with grief many people want to shut off areas of their lives, storing away emotions never to be used or hurt again.

> The bustle in a house
> The morning after death
> Is solemnest of industries
> Enacted upon earth—

The sweeping up the heart
And putting love away
We shall not want to use again
Until eternity.

Emily Dickinson

In a sense, the love we have for a given person will not be used again in the same way. Love is always fresh and new, but it is also inexhaustible. Love is an action, not something that happens to us. In helping our friends through sorrow, we want to help open new doors and fresh joys for them—so that they can feel more, not less.

Anything that will help the grieving person to know God better ministers to his real need. In sharing yourself, if you are a believer, share your faith. You can hardly do otherwise if it means anything at all to you. Friends learn from each other as they share their experiences of trusting God in life's daily emergencies, and they learn as they listen to new instruction from Him through the Scriptures. Be a catalyst for spiritual growth by the genuineness of your own excitement in knowing God. There's a comfort in getting God's point of view that can come in no other way. Pray that the sorrow of death will be used to bring your friend into a large place spiritually.

Paul wrote to the Corinthian church about God's ability to comfort us in all our afflictions so that we may be able to comfort those who are in any affliction with the comfort we ourselves have experienced (2 Corinthians 1:4). Our own adventures in God's comforts can be offered to our friends. It is authentic; it is real strength. Experiencing God's release, His answers, His healing is to grow. Growing is enriching. If sorrow produces hope, faith and love, is it not a better harvest than anxiety, bitterness and disillusionment?

In the final analysis, we offer our friendship, and the quality of our being influences others. Whether the comfort we offer in times of sorrow is genuine balm or not will depend on the quality of our personal lives. You may not feel "a natural" at offering sympathy, but you can be a natural friend and learn how to give in new ways. And what you give will one day come back to you.

CHILDREN

Little Jesus, wast Thou shy
Once, and just so small as I?
And what did it feel like to be
Out of Heaven, and just like me? . . .
Thou canst not have forgotten all
That it feels like to be small.

Francis Thompson in *Ex Ore Infantium*

— • —

A child's fresh, uncluttered innocence—and the fact of death. How does one communicate the latter to the former?

How can I tell the children that their daddy is never coming home again? All three are heavy sleepers; I opt to wait until morning to tell them. My own deep grief is upstaged by the anticipated agony of bearing this news to them. Encircled on our bed, pajama-clad, sleep and puzzlement in their eyes, they wait for me to speak. A deep breath, tears in my voice: "I have something very important to tell you. But first I want you to remember that God loves us very much, and he doesn't allow bad things to happen without being there to hold us up. A very bad thing has happened . . . ."

That's how our dear friend Mary Jane Worden told her children that their father had been killed in an automobile accident caused by a drunk driver. Who is sufficient for these things? Surely she did not feel qualified to break such news to these three innocents. But it was not unimportant how she did it. Many weeks later ten-year-old Jessie could repeat her words as though they were indelibly printed on her mind.

One could hardly bear to discuss the subject of telling children about death without the sure knowledge that God has life and death in His control. I find myself being thankful

• that God knows what it is like to be human; that he knows our scared littleness
• that the Christian name for God is *Father*
• that God calls us His children
• that He said He treasured childlike faith
• that the Bible contains the straight scoop on life and death
• that I've seen truth work in lives!

Two things every child must know to insure a healthy view of life or death: one, that he is valuable to God. "Jesus loves me this I know," is simply profound. Made in God's image, a child has worth in God's sight. God does not compare us with each other and choose the nicest. Each is made uniquely different and is special to God. The supreme worth of the individual is demonstrated by the cross. Jesus

Christ is God's way of saying, I love you enough to die for you, to take care of your sin problem and your fear of death. Every child needs to visit Calvary and have his heart transformed by God's love.

What we are talking about is evidenced in proper self-esteem. The freedom of a *loved* personality. Loved by his parents, who are God's guardians for him, yes. But something bigger: loved and accepted by God Himself, just as he is.

The cross also demonstrates God's holiness. This is the second thing a child must understand. Man's rebellion against God, our inbred tendency to sin, was so awful an offense to God's perfection that its penalty was death. He is as just as He is full of love. In the cross His justice and His love meet. He takes the penalty Himself, destroying the effects of both sin and death, for those who trust Him. Everyone needs the freedom of *forgiveness* and restored relationship.

The cross tells us we are valuable to God; the cross also demonstrates that we can never make it in either life or death without Him. From beginning to end, this is the theme of the Bible. God says, "I made you; I love you; you turned away from Me and messed up your life; I have done something about it because I love you."

This is the basic background for understanding the complexities of both life and death. We don't begin by teaching a child about death. We begin with "Who loves Patti?" And because we are God's representatives in the lives of our children, they begin to learn from us what His love means and what His character is like. Which means that we have to know ourselves; we can't teach what we haven't experienced. And we don't experience what we haven't believed. They must meet God, not our ideas about God.

That demands revelation. We cannot know Him unless He has chosen to reveal Himself. The Bible is God's revelation of His love and His character. And when it comments on the nature of man, it is a convincing diagnosis.

The obvious conclusion is this: we must read the Bible with our children if we want them to have an adequate view of God and the world. A good Bible story book could be their introduction to God. When they can read themselves, each family member should have access to a modern English translation of the Bible. In the Bible we meet goodness and evil, life and death. We see God, an all-powerful God, act on behalf of people who trust Him. We see Him transforming lives and defeating enemies. We meet Jesus Christ and see His compassion for the sick and sinful. We watch Him stop a funeral procession and restore to life the only son of the widow of Nain. He cares when people are hurt or hungry. We see Him dying—the just for the unjust—yet death has no hold over Him. We greet Easter together with fresh awe. He was dead and He is now alive!

God demonstrates His love and trustworthiness to us. In such a context, the believing heart of children handles death more capably than most adults. Children believe God can and will do what He said He would do. They let Him be God. Adults want to cut Him down to their size to make Him more understandable.

In the middle of sorrow involving the death of a close friend, participants in our conversation kept referring to the death as "an accident," implying that somehow it could have been prevented. Our seven-year-old son gave a biblical perspective to all of us. He said in his own convincing way, "I don't think you should call it an accident. It wasn't an accident. Jesus had Vince's place all ready for him in heaven and he couldn't not go just because he was in a canoe."

Imagine having your place all prepared and being unwilling to go! Where had he gotten that idea? From Jesus' words,

> Do not let your hearts be troubled. Trust in God; trust also in me. In my Father's house are many rooms; if it were not so, I would have told you. I am going there to prepare a place for you. And if I go and prepare a place for you, I will come back and take you to be with me that you also may be where I am.

John 14:1-3

Death scary? Not if it means going to God's house and being with Jesus. No wonder Jesus commented on the faith of little children.

But let's go back a step to an understanding of death. I mentioned earlier an experience of seeing a running squirrel suddenly lifeless. That's the beginning of a child's understanding. His attitude toward deadness will be conditioned by yours. You will train him.

Tell him only what you know is true. Is there a heaven for animals, for your favorite pet? We don't know. The Bible doesn't say. God made animals, so they must matter very much to Him and we can be assured that He cares. The Bible says He notices when a sparrow falls to the ground. Maybe God will have a surprise for us; but what we know for certain must be revealed to us by God in the Bible. Don't let "maybe" become a fact in your child's mind.

This is the time to talk about what makes people different from animals. People can think and talk about ideas and know about God. According to a child's age, we can speak of the distinction between body, intellect (which animals have to a degree) and spirit. We aren't just body. We can demonstrate this by looking into a mirror, because we are usually surprised that what we see is us. "I don't feel like that person," a child may say. The part of us that will live forever is our spirit, that real part of a person which can't be seen. Our bodies are the houses we live in.

When a person dies, the real part of him goes to live with God (and don't soften the biblical teaching about the necessity of personal faith) and the house he lives in, his body, is empty. It is healthier, in my opinion, to expose a child to death rather than to protect him from it. Particularly if it can be done in an unemotional context. Better, if at all possible, to meet life's great reality before it involves someone whose departure threatens personal security.

We took our third grader to the funeral of a boy our family had known. The family, including the boy, were Christians, and we knew that the man who would be conducting the service would make it a meaningful home-going for a boy whose chances for a normal life were slim from the beginning. It was a time to reaffirm, "That's not the real David. The real David has gone to be with God. That's just the house he lived in, and it is empty now." It was not morbid; our son thought David was quite privileged to go to heaven.

Opinions on exposing children to death vary, and some people would have difficulty with a situation like the one above. We traveled abroad shortly after the death of President Kennedy, and whenever we met British friends, eventually the wife got around to asking me about the "frightful" thing Mrs. Kennedy did in taking her children to the President's funeral, permitting young John to salute the casket and all. I tried to explain, without understanding English custom, that it was not uncommon in America to expose children to the reality of death and that in this particular case the Kennedy children were taking part in American history as well as their father's funeral. Later, in England, the wife of an acquaintance died, and I realized it was more typical for the British to remove the children to a relative's home and bring them back only after all the details surrounding the death were a matter of history.

While not wanting to glory in the macabre, death is a fact of life to which children must become accustomed. It was just as well not to have our child meet death for the first time when his beloved grandmother died. However, this cannot always be arranged. And if death should come without such preparation, we can still trust the mercy and healing of the same God we have known in life's other emergencies—and it is safe.

Let me return to the point of telling a child only what is true. Stories about little lost angels who look like children, and cartoons of the departed, riding clouds and playing harps—these are a lot of nonsense. We do not become angels when we die. According to the Bible, angels are a special kind of creation in God's heaven. They are God's messengers to serve Him, and Hebrews 1:14 says that in doing God's will they also minister to us.

When believers die they go to the presence of God. Jesus said to the thief on the cross who believed in Him, "Today you will be with me in paradise" (Luke 23:43). The apostle Paul said that to be absent from the body meant to be present with the Lord (2 Corinthians 5:8). When Christ comes again to complete history and take believers who are still alive out of the world, then He will give us resurrection bodies so that our whole person will be redeemed from death, including our bodies. That's why we say the body "sleeps" in death. It will be rejoined to our spirits and remade into a body that will never again know the hurts of life.

But suppose a child asks, "Did Uncle John go to heaven?" when Uncle John never gave any indication in his lifetime that he cared about God or heaven or even simple morality? Most people want to rush in with an affirmative answer even though they feel uneasy inside. I don't believe the question demands a yes or no answer. In the final analysis, who enters heaven is God's business, and we can never be certain of what has transpired in a person's inner life—or even in the last moment of life. "I don't know" is a good answer for mortals who have inadequate information.

Questions like these provide good opportunities for dialogue about what makes *anyone* worthy of heaven. The Bible says that those who have personally trusted Jesus Christ become God's children. These people demonstrate their faith by living in a vital relationship with God, trusting Him for the details of life and death. Nowhere in the Bible are we told that God keeps a list of our good and bad deeds and that if the good outweighs the bad then we are heaven-bound. Being a member of God's family is not based on good works, but on personal faith. Being God's children means we want to do what is right, but this is not to gain the status of son and daughter any more than we do what is right to earn sonship in our human family. Doing what is right is the natural product of a love relationship; we want to please God.

Because death is such a trauma in life we often entertain foggy, sentimental notions about it. Only recently I read of a woman who had an experience of feeling God was with her. She said, "Then I knew that God was also with my husband who died two years ago." That seemed like fuzzy thinking to me. Where did she think her husband was that God would be with him? Was he with *God*? is a better question. When we give wrong answers intended to soothe children, we lead them into a mist of unreality.

God's truth is comforting; our imaginative stories are not. I remember a grandmother in our town who told her grandson that his deceased father was now a star in the sky. The little boy looked across the vastness of the sky, wondering which was his father, feeling twice as lonely and forlorn as he would have if he had been told the truth.

God has a plan; our children need to know this, just as we do. We don't tell all of this at one time to a very small child any more than we tell all the facts of other parts of life at one time. We take life's situations as they come and use them to share our own knowledge of God.

A teenager suffers most when death strikes someone he loves. The insecurity of moving from childhood to adulthood, not always understanding one's self, is hard enough. When that security is further threatened by death, life can seem pretty frightening. The greater the individual's commitment to God, the more comfort is available. It is not difficult to see what a source of strength a healthy confidence in the authority of Scripture would be to such a child.

Honesty and openness are essential with teenagers. Grief must be talked about—not in forced conversations—but at sensitive moments. At such a time we need more than ever to say to each other, "I need you and you need me. I feel like you do," and so close the ranks and make life as stable as possible.

"What was my dad like?" Any child who has lost a parent at an early age wonders what relationship he missed, what model for life she never knew. A son wonders if he is like his father or what advice his father might have given him in a perplexing situation. In our struggle to find our own identity we need to know our heritage.

While this "wondering" is plaguing the child, a parent may be building a new life—not without important memories, but with a determination to live in the present and make life meaningful. The parent knows the past; the child does not. A wise parent takes walks into the past with a child to acquaint him with the people he needs to know. This is true for parents and grandparents in particular. Introducing deceased brothers and sisters needs special sensitivity so that the lost sibling doesn't become a monster rival of unrealistic goodness and perfection. But we need to know who we belong to!

In counseling university students over the years I am impressed with the importance of parents facing their children's loss with a linguistic solution. Talk. Share memories, the small moments which enrich a child's self-understanding. A child recognizes the implications of his loss years after parents have coped with their own sorrow. When parents are a closed box about the past, a teenager's identity crisis seems to heighten.

Only recently a university girl shared with me her personal anxiety about her relationships with boys, her tremendous need to belong to someone and some of her unwise judgments about what made a relationship valid. Discussing her life situation, I discovered that her father had died when she was eight years old. She had been her daddy's little girl. Another father replaced him two years later, but at the age of ten she couldn't make the transfer of relationship, not the same kind of relationship she had before. She was still looking for a place of safety in her daddy's lap! When I said this to her, we proceeded into new areas of understanding herself and her needs. Her mother could have helped her see this a long time ago if she had been aware of her daughter's needs and had been more open to verbalizing the past. Some areas of life are made more secure and decidedly richer by remembering!

It is great to be acquainted with a God who has access to our children's hearts as well as our own. All of life's answers are found in Him. He is not limited by life's circumstances. He can reach down into a little child's heart or the heart of a silent teenager and provide just the right comfort. He can do that even when people aren't sure they want him to do it.

RITUALS

We brought nothing into the world, and we can take nothing out of it.

Paul's first letter to Timothy

THE MEMORIAL SERVICE for Dick was wonderfully Christian and comforting. We sang several hymns throughout the service, chosen carefully by Marilyn, with words so true and real they made our spirits soar while at the same time leaving us tender inside. The children placed the pall embroidered with a cross over the casket as the minister spoke of its symbolism: Dick covered by the death of Jesus Christ. Three people spoke about Dick; one of them was his son John. Again the comments were simple, true and often humorous. We were laying to rest a real man with human foibles, but as John said, "His weaknesses made him trust the Lord the more." The pastor said he had never known a man so certain he was going home to be with the Lord . . . .

(from my journal)

— • —

*D*eath is not beautiful. The undertaker's cleverest handiwork cannot make it so. At death the body becomes an empty tent, the abandoned house where someone once lived—cold, lifeless, mortal. The sting of death is real; it will disappear only when mortality puts on immortality, when the corruptible puts on incorruption.

Death occurs; a loved one is gone; a body remains. In that one sentence are the cold, hard facts of life. The stunning grief, the shock of the loss are enough. Yet a body remains. We cannot fool ourselves. In one sense we know the body is worthless without the spirit, yet it is the physical expression of the person we knew. It, therefore, has dignity and a value identified with our own value. What to do with the body is a problem which has faced humankind since death began, and the rituals surrounding death, different in each culture, have evolved from this uncomfortable necessity.

And perhaps it is a hidden mercy. If the body were swept away at the moment of death, the event would seem even more unreal. The body is a reminder of a grim reality. Death takes some getting used to, and the details surrounding death's arrangements can be part of learning to live with the facts. An unrecovered body in the event of death often leaves the bereaved at loose ends, as if they wished for a final act to perform.

Funerals or memorial services are a way to care for the body of deceased ones. But they are also for us. Whatever the ritual we perform, we do it partly to verify the dignity and importance of living in the face of the indignity of death. Most people have thought very little about the history of contemporary practices. Death occurs and the bereaved are swept along into a prevailing custom without realizing what they are doing, why they are doing it, or if they want to do it that way.

Over the centuries, in a variety of cultures, handling the body of the dead has run the gamut from funerary extravagance (the embalming of Egypt) to the quickest possible disposal of the body (Hindu burning ghats and contemporary cremation).

In early America taking care of the dead was a family affair. People died at home. Family members or close friends washed and laid out the body; a local carpenter constructed the coffin; the church sexton had the grave dug; the service was held in the church or in the home. With friends and relatives present, the body was laid in the church graveyard, a meaningful reminder of Christian hope.

In the primitive life of frontier areas, death held even more intimate involvements—unmarked graves in untracked areas, dug by a husband or a son, the simple service spoken by a family member or friend. No camouflage for death here.

Times change. In the 1900s life became "nicer," partly because of the industrialization of our country. Large segments of the population moved to cities; people needed and could afford more help in burying their dead. The role of the modern funeral director is a relatively recent one. Even as late as 1900 embalming was an exception rather than a rule. As affluence increased, the public's expectation of what a funeral director must perform also grew. Fancier hearses for the common man, more elaborate ceremonial touches and, as the details of death moved away from the church and family, the posh funeral home became part of a cultural expectation.

The vast societal changes ushered in by the industrial revolution could not help but affect all areas of life. "Scientific thought" made man feel more capable, more able to control his destiny, and less dependent on God. In Europe the higher critical approach to Scripture swept the continent in the later 1800s. By the early 1900s it had spread to America, casting doubt on the reliability of scriptural revelation, moving off-center of the message of hope and peace. Glorying in man, the religious establishment focused on man's ability to solve man's problems. Huge segments of the church no longer had a convincing word for either life or death.

Dying increasingly became an embarrassing concept in a society where few knew the answer to death. People began to look to the funeral director for the help they had once received from the church and the community. And where death cannot be faced, it must be obscured as much as possible. Thus some of our contemporary customs carry an aura of death-denial about them.

When death's reality must be obscured, there are two ways to do it: 1) apply make-up to the body of the deceased, clothe it in finery, give it the best of everything—to glory in the body with a kind of extravagance designed to defy death; or 2) dispose of the body as quickly as possible, avoid the corpse, remove from the scene that hideous reality. Death obscured, repressed or swiftly dismissed reflects the mindset of the living, rather than that of the funeral director. Decisions made about the dead will vary according to the ability and sensitivity of those making them.

Many a man, concerned about the high cost of dying, has remarked to his wife, "When I die, just put me in a pine box and bury me the same day. Forget about all the fancy finery. It's not me anymore, it's just a lump of clay." Or maybe it's a suggestion for cremation. Whatever, the emphasis is on the inexpensive and the unpretentious.

Taken superficially that sounds sensible. Especially if a person has witnessed extravagantly emotional displays that were more death-denying than death-affirming. But it isn't that simple on several counts.

"Pine box" equals a simple wooden casket in most people's mind—the simplicity of wood, no adornment. But the "simplest" wooden casket available is second in expense to a bronze casket. Unless you can hire a carpenter to put together a pine box, you'll have to be content with a cloth-covered wooden casket.

Whether it is a burial or a cremation—with today's involved processes of opening a grave, installing a vault, getting medical releases—burying a person "the same day" is not as easy as it sounds. Cremation is a quicker removal of the body, but its actual cremation is not always immediate. I mention these details only to point out that we often don't have facts to back up our most earnest statements.

But there are more important considerations than these. What is the Christian view of the body? It is at this point that we need to think through a Christian philosophy for the care of the dead.

Throughout the Bible, the body is seen as good—an instrument for the expression of personality. For fullness of life a person needs a body. That seems a facetious statement until we remember that God also says we need a body for the life ahead of us. We will not be disembodied spirits throughout eternity. The Scripture says clearly that our bodies will be raised incorruptible, no longer subject to decay. "He who raised Christ from the dead will also give life to your mortal bodies" (Romans 8:11). We affirm this great truth each time we say the Apostles' Creed, "I believe in the resurrection of the body . . . ."

The Christian view of the body is unique in the world. The Greeks thought that the body was evil. Plato speaks of the body as an impediment in the search for true being. In the *Phaedo* he quotes Socrates as saying that in the life to come we shall get rid of the foolishness of the body and be pure. George Bernard Shaw picks up this heresy in *Man and Superman* and speaks of escaping this tyranny of the flesh, of being a ghost, an appearance, an illusion . . . in a word, bodiless. Eastern religions hold this same low view of the body and of all matter. And early Christian ascetics, confused by the biblical instruction to reject the "works of the flesh," fell into this error when they thought this meant they must deny the body.

But Christ teaches plainly that evil comes from the heart of a man, from his inner desires. The body is good. What we do, therefore, with our bodies has always been important to God. He refers to a Christian's body as the temple of the Holy Spirit. Our bodies are so important they will be raised from the dead!

It seems fitting then, that at death, the body should be treated with the respect and dignity which reflects the value of personhood. We reject the idea of dumping dead bodies in the street like ordinary rubbish as happened in the sweeping terror of ancient plagues. The dignity of man in life necessitates some comparable dignity in death—not so much for the sake of the dead person, but for those who are still alive and feel the attachment of their personhood to that of the deceased. At death we reaffirm the worth of the total individual.

In the Bible when the patriarch Jacob died, he gave a charge to his sons:

> I am about to be gathered to my people. Bury me with my fathers in the cave in the field of Ephron the Hittite, the cave in the field of Machpelah, near Mamre in Canaan, which Abraham bought as a burial place from Ephron the

Hittite, along with the field. There Abraham and his wife
Sarah were buried, there Isaac and his wife Rebekah were
buried, and there I buried Leah . . . .

Genesis 49:29-31

When Jacob died, his sons carried out these specific
instructions, a large entourage leaving Egypt to go to the
plain of Mamre. Since he died in the land of Egypt, his son
Joseph, who was a high official in Egypt's government,
followed the Egyptian practice of embalming in an otherwise
Hebrew family funeral.

When it came Joseph's time to die he spoke to his sons,
saying, "I am about to die. But God will surely come to your
aid and take you up out of this land to the land he promised
on oath to Abraham, Isaac and Jacob . . . and then you must
carry my bones up from this place." Four hundred years later
when Moses led the exodus of Israel's children from Egypt's
bondage, they remembered and took Joseph's remains with
them.

This same respect was shown to the body of Jesus Christ
when His disciples took it from the cross, prepared it for
burial and laid it in Joseph's tomb. The specific customs of
embalming or the use of spices may be cultural; the care for a
person's body is not.

William Gladstone is quoted as saying, "Show me the
manner in which a nation or community cares for its dead,
and I will measure with mathematical exactness the character
of its people, their respect for laws of the land, and their
loyalty to high ideals." Although he was neither an
anthropologist nor a sociologist, Gladstone's comment
simply amplifies that attitudes toward death and practices at
the time of death evidence the quality of group life.

Jessica Mitford in her popular criticism of American funerals, *The American Way of Death*, refers to the "fullfledged burlesque of the funeral industry," and when a funeral fits that description, it does reflect the value structure of the people involved. The way the living handle death is a statement of their view of the unique value of the deceased, as well as their own value. Death is always more than a biological event or nature's planned obsolescence.

Obviously the treatment given his body does a dead man no good. It is simple folly to believe that a delay in decay by an airtight casket or a vacuum-sealed vault is of any value. Flesh decays. It should and it will. Job faced squarely the fact that worms would destroy his body. A body which returns to the dust is no more a problem to God, when it comes to resurrection, than a body burned in cremation or eaten by vultures. "All flesh is as grass . . . ."

Another consideration necessary to realistically handle the "pine box" theory involves our mental health in facing reality. The anguish of grief is real. Death comes as a terrifying blow. It is not easy to get used to. I would not view lightly the value of a waiting period between death and funeral or memorial services as a valuable time to experience the support of friends and loved ones and get used to the fact of death. In Jewish tradition where the body is buried within a short time, the family and friends gather for a daily prescribed period of mourning. Many psychiatrists support the theory that death rituals are not cruel exploitations, but necessary grief therapy. Obviously circumstances temper our needs. Sometimes there is no body to dispose of at all, and death seems unreal, almost as if those behind are waiting for the event to be completed. In another instance, a lingering illness may have prepared the family for loss, and death comes as a strange mixture of relief and sorrow. Psychological needs vary, and in the shock of grief, we are not always sure what our needs are. Most burial rituals have come into being as an expression of some need the living have to experience group help in coming to terms with the grief they face—a need which has only begun to be met by the rituals.

For a growing number of Americans cremation is seen as a way to reduce costs and simplify arrangements while allowing for suitable memorialization of the dead. It is an ancient practice and is steadily gaining in popularity. During the past ten years, for example, the proportion of people cremated upon death has risen from seven to fourteen percent of the total who die each year. In some states the figure exceeds twenty-five percent. Some families choose to bury their own dead and make the arrangements that comply with state public health requirements. Only a few states require that a funeral director supervise such arrangements.

Grief therapy is no small thing. We cannot simply close off rooms in our heart like closing a door in our house. If a person cannot weep at loss, something is strung up too tightly inside of him. Tears are not weakness; they are God's plan for emotional release. Anxiety is compounded when efforts are made to deny the depth of death's impact. Probably the times of greatest emotional need in human life are during infancy and when death occurs.

English anthropologist Geoffrey Gorer, in his book *Death, Grief and Mourning,* comments at length about community help in enduring grief. In studying the behavior of those who try to ignore their feelings of grief, he says, "I had the feeling that, by denying expression of their grief, they had reduced their lives to triviality . . . to meaningless 'busyness' through the private rituals of what I have called mummification to the apathy of despair . . . ."

Surely any public service held at the time of death does

not end the time of mourning, but studies seem to confirm that community help in expressing grief is healthy and that a time for public mourning helps a family face the most acute type of deprivation they will encounter.

Viewing the body is the custom most subject to debate. Again, I believe this depends on the needs of the living. A corpse is an affirmation of death's reality. But a closed casket affirms the same with quiet dignity and privacy in death. Yet for some, viewing the body relieves their personal threat of death. Everyone has a feeling for his own body and viewing a dead body may curiously reassure the person about the value, the aliveness of his own body. On the other hand a neurotic refusal to view a body could mean an inability to admit the fact of death and our anxiety about it. In between these are a variety of emotions and personal convictions. The decision must be a family decision based again on personal need and conviction, rather than on public opinion. That is why it is well to think through a personal philosophy ahead of time.

I do not believe one practice is more Christian than another. The attitude which surrounds the custom is of primary importance.

It seems obvious, but it bears repeating—any ritual surrounding death is not for the dead, but for the living. In paying respect to the dead person we are telling the remaining loved ones that we valued the deceased and we care about the living. When the display of the dead body becomes more the focus of sympathy calls than the grieving family, something is amiss in our value structure. (For this reason, if the casket is open, it would help if the viewing room were separate from the place where a visitor meets the living members of the family.) We are not there to glorify a dead body. As my own minister commented, "It is more important to look the widow in the face and share sincere sympathy than to look at the corpse and comment on how natural he looks." Something insecure in us rivets our attention away from the need of the living to focus on the body of the deceased when it is the center of the encounter. Anyone sensitive to human need knows that viewing the body is not synonymous with offering sympathy and comfort.

In smaller cities and rural areas, families do not greet friends in the funeral home. Everyone knows where the bereaved family lives and comes to their home to make calls. In urban areas, increasingly friends call on the family at the funeral home and do not take time off from work to attend the actual funeral service. Regardless of the circumstances, it is the sympathy of friends and their physical presence with us that offers the human support we need.

We live in a rapidly changing society with human needs which remain fairly constant. Our customs need to be open to scrutiny and reevaluation, and the fast pace of contemporary life will augment new patterns of behavior. Already the mobility of life has given people a sense of rootlessness and has destroyed strong family cohesiveness. Death, without the emotional investment and care of other family members, can be an incredibly lonely experience. When dying is given an increasingly impersonal and unimportant quality, in turn life itself seems more unimportant and impersonal. Some of our present practices may become altered simply from the lack of consensus regarding what it means to be human and vulnerable. This is a dangerous situation if the changes do not take into consideration a person's psychological and spiritual needs.

Our society has both the freedom and need to examine afresh what a Christian funeral should be, but not without great sensitivity to what is already happening sociologically in

our country. The move against the structural monopoly of
the funeral establishment in controlling the ritual of death
may be legitimate, but a ritual there will be. We need to take
care that in disposing of one ritual we do not take up another
which minimizes human values.

Robert Fulton, in his book *Death and Identity*, makes a
relevant observation about the shift in societal structure.

> The denial of death and deritualization of mourning
> growing apace in America today parallel and reflect other
> significant changes apparent in family life. These changes
> can be identified briefly as: 1) from predominance of the
> religious to predominance of the secular, 2) from a large
> group to a small group, 3) from a stable to a mobile group,
> 4) from an adult-centered to a child-centered family, 5)
> from a communal family ideology to a democratic one, 6)
> from an integrated to an individualized group, and 7) from
> a neighborhood-enclosed family to an isolated family in an
> urban environment.

The church increasingly needs to be the stabilizer of
family life, offering community strength to wavering human
need. If the church fulfills its commission it will be pressed
into more and more involvement in both matters of life and
death. The pressures of life will demand it. And perhaps
from the church will come a distinctly Christian way to
handle the ceremonies of death in a pagan society which are
different from any we know now.

The Christian way of death takes man's needs seriously.
The Christian message speaks openly to real people about
real things; it is not an escape device. Hence, the Christian
way of death should give evidence of the value of the body,
the integrity of individuality, the honesty of grief, and the
hope beyond the sorrow. Whatever ritual is used, and

customs vary within Christianity and within our own country, Christian burial is not a time of denial but of reaffirmation.

A Christian funeral or memorial service is one that expresses Christian hope. The community of the living support the remaining loved ones with concern and sympathy. It affirms the uniqueness of individual personality and the social character of human existence. In a world that is essentially materialistic, a Christian funeral gives a strong statement of faith in that which cannot be seen. It is an acceptance of reality, of deep feelings and a restatement of truths which give meaning to life.

A Christian funeral does not equate the worth of an individual with the expense of the casket or the number of floral pieces. Indeed, the Christian view points away from ostentatious display to spiritual reality. The more recent trend to substitute memorial funds for perishable flowers makes sense to the Christian. A Christian funeral is a statement of hope, not a final social event. Some churches drape the casket with a pall during the service, minimizing its quality, making all persons equal in death. The use of a pall is particularly significant when, marked with a cross, it symbolizes that the deceased places his hope of eternal life in the work of Christ on the cross. A Christian funeral does more to speak to the question of death than to eulogize the deceased, and uses the Scriptures to offer comfort. How alive biblical truths become in the face of death!

Some Practical Considerations

Willing one's body for medical research is growing in popularity. If not the whole body, vital organs can be given which offer new hope to the living. A Christian view would support either of these plans, although this is the kind of personal decision which should have the support of the closest loved ones. Plans must be made ahead of time. A certificate bequeathing the body or parts thereof for medical research must be signed in advance, and can be obtained from your lawyer. Research centers vary in their need for bodies and in what contributions they agree to make to transportation and burial costs.

Arrangements ought to be made on other levels of funeral planning as well. Personal wishes should be expressed and written down after some research has been done. Preplanning forms are available and can be filed with a funeral director, but it is also adequate to have these instructions written down at home if other family members are informed of the location of such papers.

At the time of death those making arrangements often find it difficult to do so. Sometimes people don't even know a funeral director to call. Most have limited experience in choosing caskets and vaults and making decisions regarding finances for funeral arrangements. We need to turn to the church instead of the funeral home for help in decision-making and funeral planning. Ministers, who are fulfilling a pastoral role, are informed about services available, about reputable firms and adequate burial plans. I asked funeral directors about how often ministers help in making arrangements, and found it to be surprisingly seldom. Yet I do know of the wise counsel ministers have given widows of meager means in making arrangements. Love and sorrow combined can produce poor judgment in financial responsibility, especially if an element of guilt is present. A man who genuinely does the work of a pastor will not usurp family rights or privacy, but he is a more objective source of help. Personally, I would also like to see funeral/memorial services return to the church if the church has been an important factor in the life of the deceased.

In the final analysis, a Christian funeral is not determined by cost or efficiency, but by the message it proclaims. Here are the believing ones, made in the image of God, taking death's penalty seriously, but without the sorrow of those who have no hope. Here is the community of those who fear God, caring for the living, mourning the loss of the dead. The Christian way of death is not given to the showmanship of self-indulgence or material values; it is a statement to the world about where our real home is.

And in a day when death remains man's unconquerable foe, in the face of our vast scientific accomplishment, the Christian's expression of hope and immortality in the presence of death is a shining light in a dark world. People need to be reminded that they are on their way home.

GOD

GOD IS FATHER; He is my Father. As Father He is the Originator, the Source of all that is. As Father He is also Redeemer, my Redeemer, the Safe Place, El Shaddai, the God who is enough.

God is the Great Innovator, bringing to fruition all that is His pleasure. Limitless in knowledge and power, He is the great Lion who devours kings and kingdoms. Yet He is also the One who intervenes so that a widow who trusts Him has her son restored or finds the cruse of oil does not run dry.

He is the One who first loved so that I might know what love is all about. He is the One who gave the eye, the ear, the mind, and the aesthetic sense that causes me to reach out beyond my human smallness to rejoice in a sunset and comprehend a beautiful piece of music. He is the Source of all wisdom and joy.

I stand in awe of His holiness. I cannot comprehend the vastness of it, the quality of it. How can One so terrible in justice and holiness be at the same time so rich in love and mercy? Yet I experience the reality of His grace, His forgiveness, His love—the safeness of knowing Him. His righteous judgments terrify me; His love overwhelms me.

The completeness of His forgiveness breaks my proud self.

As a child I used to picture myself sitting on God's lap, safely tucked in the circle of His loving arms. I knew He was the Judge, that He worked in the world beyond and through the evil He found there and that He knew everything. But He loved me. Intellectually I know God is a Spirit, that He has no lap. Emotionally my reactions to Him have not left the safety of childhood. His sovereignty and His Fatherhood have been my delights.

I meet God in Jesus Christ. He is the One who can weep at Lazarus's death and then by His Power, the Power which holds the universe together, bring Lazarus back from the dead. He is the One who never compromises truth because He is Truth. At the same time He is full of grace, because He is Grace.

I cannot think up to Him, least of all beyond Him. So He has come to me, revealing Himself according to my capacity, lovingly at work in the small details of my life, while at the same time ruling as the Sovereign of all creation. God is beyond my descriptions; He is beyond my experience of Him. But this I know, He is my Father.

(from my journal)

— • —

*W*hat comes into your mind when you think about God is the most important thing about you. It determines your spiritual future and the way you live in the present.

If I were to ask you to take ten minutes and write down who God is to you, what would you write?

It is not an irrelevant question. The issues of life and

death hang on the character of God. The person who comes to a right belief about God is the freest of men. Myriads of temporal problems and perplexities about eternity fall off his back. He no longer carries the weight of responsibility for a world he cannot control. He is content to let God be God.

It is not our ideas about God, but God who matters. The importance of expressing what we think about God is only to reveal what is rubble in our thinking and what is true. The real God often lies buried in the heap of wrong ideas we've collected about Him. Does it matter if we know the real God? Infinitely. We can never know who or what we are until we know something of God. Our ground of existence is linked to Him. The most serious question in life is God Himself. In the religions of the world men seek after God; in Christianity we have God seeking men and revealing His character to them. We are not groping in the dark; we are living in the light of revelation.

People often want to reduce God to manageable terms. That is why we hear and say arrogant things like "I can't conceive of a God who . . . ." Or "Why does God put up with . . . ?" Or "I don't think God would . . . ." We think beyond ourselves only with great difficulty. God is infinitely beyond us. He is incomprehensible and unapproachable. Yet He has revealed Himself in the Scriptures and become infinitely near in Jesus Christ. If the lesser would know the greater, the greater must disclose Himself. Amazingly, the eternal God, the Creator, has done this. He is the Initiator. It is so staggering that some will not believe it.

The revelation of God strains language. That is why the Bible uses *like* or *the likeness of*—because the revelation must be one human beings can understand. God has disclosed His character to us in the history of the Old Testament, always promising to intervene in human history with salvation. The story of the New Testament is summed up by John:

> The Word [Jesus Christ] became flesh and made his dwelling among us. We have seen his glory, the glory of the One and Only, who came from the Father, full of grace and truth.
>
> No one has ever seen God, but God the One and Only, who is at the Father's side, has made him known.
>
> John 1:14, 18

What is the nature of God's character? When we read God is love that does not simply mean that He acts lovingly. That God is love is a fact, not a definition. It is what He is. This is true of all His attributes. God is love. His love knows no bounds. God is constant. He is in His essential being whatever attributes He has disclosed to us—and He is in perfect harmony. Nothing in God is more or less, great or small. He is simply God. He is what He is in Himself. How comforting to turn from our limitations to a God who has none.

This knowledge led Moses to sing

> Lord, you have been our dwelling place throughout all generations. Before the mountains were born or you brought forth the earth and the world, from everlasting to everlasting you are God.
>
> Psalm 90:1-2

God is all-wise. His wisdom sees everything in focus. He is able to work toward an eternal plan with precision, not deterred by the waywardness of men. Nothing takes Him by surprise; He never wonders what He will do. He is all-knowing. No one can inform Him about us or tattle any secret to Him. He knows us completely. He knows our frailty, our potential, our affliction.

God is good. The goodness and love of God mean that He has charged Himself with full responsibility for our lives and is willing to take over management if we turn to Him. God, in being love and goodness, has planned for our highest good. The wisdom of God plans it; the power of God achieves it, and He is kind.

> "Though the mountains be shaken and the hills be removed, yet my unfailing love for you will not be shaken nor my covenant of peace be removed," says the LORD, who has compassion on you.
>
> Isaiah 54:10

God is faithful; He is constant. He is the same yesterday, today and forever. We don't have to wonder how He will react today, what mood He will be in tomorrow morning. He is constant in all His attributes—constant in His justice, goodness, wisdom and power—because these are facets of the essential nature of God. God does not change in His concern for people; He never tires or loses His enthusiasm for what He has begun. "I the LORD do not change" (Malachi 3:6)!

Read Isaiah 40 and absorb the wonder of His being.

> Do you not know? Have you not heard? The LORD is the everlasting God, the Creator of the ends of the earth. He will not grow tired or weary, and his understanding no one can fathom.
>
> Isaiah 40:28

This trustworthiness of God's behavior in His world has made scientific truth possible. Scientific "laws" are simply observations of God's faithfulness.

God is omnipresent. He is everywhere, always near. That is a great truth to put to work in life. God's presence knows no geographical or spatial limits—up, down, across and beyond. The reality of this truth was impressed simply on me one weekend when we left our little son with friends. He was so glad to see us when we returned and clung so tightly that I began to question the wisdom of ever having left. But then a small voice spoke a great truth, "Know what? God can be every place. He was here with me and He was away with you." God is in the far-flung places of the earth. He is infinitely near. No son or daughter, no husband or wife—no one can go where He is not. Read Psalm 139.

God is holy—holiness beyond our imagination. Holy is the way God is. He does not conform to a standard; He is the standard. He is sovereign. He is perfectly just.

The harmony, the perfection, the splendor, the creativity within the character of God tell us that God is joy. Gladness, mirth, joyfulness beyond measure spring out of the very nature of God. When He spoke in creation, the morning stars sang together. He touches a person's life and puts a song of praise in the heart. The psalmist could sing of "God, my joy and my delight" (Psalm 43:4), and reiterate, "You will fill me with joy in your presence" (Psalm 16:11). Joy is a heavenly commodity; it exists in full measure wherever God is. It has even caused men to sing at a graveside. That is why Jesus said He came to earth "that they may have the full measure of my joy within them" (John 17:13).

All that God does must be in accord with what God is. He cannot act out of character. He is who He is. Justice is present in mercy; love is present in justice. His will and His love are the same.

We rest in what God is—and find His character vastly comforting. This one is the God of all comfort. Faith is confidence in the character of God.

We see this God move into the pages of the New Testament and meet Him in Jesus Christ. We see afresh that all the promises of God are yes in Jesus Christ. In a conversation with His disciples, Jesus said, "If you really knew me, you would know my Father as well . . . . Anyone who has seen me has seen the Father" (John 14:7, 9).

Christ moves among men in holiness, in goodness. He is tenderhearted and sympathetic. He listens to men, He comes to them—not because He is indebted to them, but because He is merciful.

> He doth give His joy to all:
> He becomes an infant small,
> He becomes a man of woe,
> He doth feel the sorrow too.
> Think not thou canst sigh a sigh,
> And thy Maker is not by:
> Think not thou canst weep a tear,
> And thy Maker is not near.

William Blake

He is forgiving, considerate, hospitable, kind. We see Him and come to love Him. Fear toward God is turned to faith; love casts out fear. Faith is standing in awe of who God is and not being afraid.

We have only skimmed the surface of the infinite character of God. The Bible tells us much more than this, yet all that can be said of His trinity, His self-existence, His self-sufficiency, His eternity is beyond us. What we have seen is enough to know that our experience of Him has only begun.

I have said before that all our peace in this life and in death hangs on the character of God. He has told us who He is. Our lack of faith reflects not on His character, but on ours. Faith is confidence that what He says is true.

Recently in a group discussion on the eighth chapter of the book of Romans, a young widow shared her own experience with us. In her girlhood she had discovered Romans 8:28 and the following verses which affirm that nothing is able to separate us from the love of God in Jesus Christ. That chapter became her favorite. Years passed and life was rich and full. When her husband was suddenly killed everything good seemed to end. Her minister came to comfort her and asked if she had any favorite Bible passage she would like him to read with her. She mentioned Romans 8, and listened with new awareness as he read,

> And we know that in all things God works for the good of those who love him, who have been called according to his purpose.

They had been favorite words to her in a superficial sense. It had been easy to say them and to believe them before. Now her life lay in shambles; the beauty was all gone. Could it still be her favorite verse? Could she still say, *I know . . . God works for good?*

She had tested it with time, and we waited to hear her conclusion. The words came out between tears, but what she said was genuine. Yes, it is true, she said, I know that in *everything* God works for good.

She does not understand what happened or why. She simply has turned instead to what she knows of the goodness of God, to the reliability of His character—to God Himself.

Darkness to the intellect
But sunshine to the heart.

I speak to myself. I have not faced death's worst dissolution of my life. Will "the rope" hold in such a day? I feel such human reluctance to give up anyone I love. I feel the fear of life without them. And yet, having said that, I know from every past experience that God is utterly trustworthy, that in the wonder of all that He is, He will take the pieces of my life and work for my good. I rest in what God is.

Some years ago I did the exercise I recommended earlier in this chapter. I wrote down my scattered thoughts about the character of God. I shared them at the beginning of this chapter to emphasize that knowing the God of all comfort is a personal matter. Facts about God are not enough; it is relationship with God that is infinitely comforting.

Jesus Christ spoke of this relationship in the Sermon on the Mount. In discussing the anxieties so common to men, He said, "Don't be anxious. Your heavenly Father knows . . . ." *Your heavenly Father.* A truth so obvious, so intimate: the Christian name for God is Father. Surely the Fatherhood of God is at the core of the universe.

If you have ever seen the care, the grace, the peace and the joy the heavenly Father gives those who trust Him, even when life has been shattered, you will know what I have been saying is true. This quality life cannot be denied as forcible evidence that God is beyond both life and death.

Out of the struggle of his soul, George Matheson, the blind poet and scholar, wrote the familiar hymn,

> O Love that wilt not let me go,
> I rest my weary soul in Thee;
> I give Thee back the life I owe,
> That in Thine ocean depths its flow
> May richer, fuller be.

There is no other comfort like the comfort given by the God of all comfort.

I have not said it all nor said it well. Just as God is beyond us and yet deigns to come to us, so death is beyond our understanding and will surely come to us. But whatever in our lives has been good and "yes" comes to us because of that first glorious fact of God.

Our deepest joys only emphasize the transience of life and create in us a wistfulness for something more, as if they are a foretaste of what in larger measure would really satisfy our inner thirst. A nostalgia beckons us to God, awakens us to life beyond this one. An inconsolable longing which no experience in life quite satisfies reminds us that we were made for another world.

In *The Problem of Pain*, C. S. Lewis concluded:

> There have been times when I think we do not desire heaven, but more often I find myself wondering whether, in our heart of hearts, we have ever desired anything else . . . . It is the secret signature of each soul, the incommunicable and unappeasable want . . . .
>
> All your life an unattainable ecstasy has hovered just beyond the grasp of your consciousness. The day is coming when you will awake to find, beyond all hope, that you have attained it . . . . "

And you will have come home.

Note to the Reader

The publisher invites you to share your response to the message of this book by writing Discovery House Publishers, P.O. Box 3566, Grand Rapids, MI 49501 U.S.A. or by calling 800-283-8333. For information about other Discovery House publications, contact us at the same address and phone number.